LIFE AFTER COLLEGE

SO YOU GRADUATED ...NOW WHAT?

DIANE LENTO-McGOVERN

Betterway Publications, Inc.

White Hall, Virginia

Published by Betterway Publications, Inc.
Box 77
White Hall, VA 22987

Cover design by Deborah C. Chappell
Typography by Typecasting

Library of Congress Cataloging-in-Publication Data

Lento–McGovern, Diane
    Life after college.

    Bibliography: p. 171.
    Included index.
    1. Vocational guidance.   2. College graduates —
Employment. 3. Universities and colleges — Graduate
work. 4. Job hunting. I. Title.
HF5381.L354   1987   331.7′02   87–6412
ISBN 0-932620-77-9 (pbk.)

Printed in the United States of America
0 9 8 7 6 5 4 3 2 1

To
Norma and Jim
for obvious reasons...

To
Christopher
for not so obvious reasons.

A Special Thanks To...

Richard Scott. Jeanne Scott. Bob and Jackie Hostage. Sue Burrows. Jim and Norma Lento. Christopher. My friends and family. Everyone I interviewed. And all who offered advice and support.

CONTENTS

PART I.

1.
SO YOU GRADUATED FROM COLLEGE... NOW WHAT?

Graduating from college can bring you down to earth fast. No longer can you postpone those tough decisions about your future. It's time to solve questions such as: "Should I apply to law school?" "Look for a job?" "Join the merchant marine?" "Should I tour the country?" "Start my own business?" "Become a rock star?" Perhaps you've eliminated a couple of these choices. Maybe you've added more. Whichever the case, many of you are now compelled to make lifetime decisions such as these, yet you don't feel quite ready.

I can sympathize. Not long ago, as my graduation approached, I had a lot of ideas about what to do next: I had just completed a great internship and considered looking for a job in the recording industry. I thought of taking advantage of my freedom and traveling across the country. I dreamt about getting a doctorate, but had no idea what to study. I was caught in a whirlpool of indecision. As I wondered about music school, questioned the Peace Corps and considered business, I became more and more frantic thinking I was the only person confused. There was med school, Europe to travel and a world of knowledge untapped. There were management programs, the armed services, work studies abroad. Almost everything and anything seemed to be available to me. Yet the day I graduated from college, there was nothing I wanted more than to have someone else plan my future.

And why not? I wasn't the kind of student being groomed for a family business. I wasn't ready for one of the "big eight" accounting firms. Nor was I hoping to ever win an Academy Award. I was a bewildered eighteen-year-old who went to college hoping to find my niche. But I graduated even more confused with an awareness of an even longer list of options. Recently I interviewed a Franklin and Marshall graduate who hit it right on target. He said, "First of all, I entered college as a teenager not knowing much about the real world. The things I thought wouldn't interest me usually became more appealing as I learned about them. And the things I held as dreams usually lost their flavor as I saw how they were affected by politics, economy, society and religion. It's no wonder graduation was traumatic for me.

I just wish I had known everyone else was just as confused as I was."

That's exactly why I wrote *Life After College*. It's for people who don't know what they want and aren't sure of all their options. It's for people who think they know what they want but aren't sure how to get it. And it's for people who have very definite goals and have already started to pursue them. (I should underline this last group, since people who are set in their ways often overlook important options. For instance, you may be surprised to find that a liberal arts graduate most likely has the prerequisites for medical school. This means virtually any college graduate with good grades has a shot at med school entrance exams. Imagine an English major incorporating his communication skills with his medical practice? Not only would he be better equipped to help his patients describe their symptoms, he'd be able to explain the diagnosis and treatment more effectively.)

Life After College is for students and graduates who are confused by too much advice like the following:

"Immediately look for a job after graduating."

"It's better to work for a large company."

"Grad school is the way to go."

"It's who you know that really counts."

"Become proficient in a foreign language so you have special hooks to lure an employer."

The list is endless.

Life After College is for students who told me:

"Sometimes the best time spent is time spent doing nothing. This is usually when I decide what it is I want."

"I try to be open to suggestions."

"I like to try new things."

"I'm young. I have time to change."

"I don't want to limit myself."

This book is for these open-minded individuals because it serves as a guide to most options available and shows how to go about choosing and obtaining them.

Life After College is for students who graduated at the top of their class, the lower half and everywhere in between. It's for graduates who want a job, prefer to travel or plan to go to graduate school. It's for capitalists, humanitarians and people who are just plain confused.

All in all, *Life After College* is for the homogenized group of college graduates Auren Uris and John Tarrant describe in their book *Career Stages*[1]. The authors claim if you combine a healthy cross section of college students you'll be able to classify each into one of the following categories: got-it-together people, passive–dependent people, railroad-track people, side-road wanderers and the walking wounded. Although

---

[1] Auren Uris and John Tarrant, *Career Stages (New York: Seaview/Putnam, 1983), pp. 35–36.*

the authors use their categories to show how graduates approach the job market, the categories also serve as good delineators of how graduates face the real world:

• *Got-it-together people.* They're aware of their skills and talents, know the direction in which they're headed and seek the best route possible.

• *Passive-dependent people.* They're a little unrealistic, have to be guided along step-by-step, have skills and talents but are unclear how to market or profit from them.

• *Railroad-track people.* They're very directed, are pretty sure how to get what they want, and are looking for the best place or best way to develop themselves.

• *Side-road wanderers.* They have no definite goals or aspirations, are people who don't strain themselves. They just go along with the flow.

• *The walking wounded.* More than merely seeking advice, they depend almost entirely on people for moral and emotional support. Usually they are marginally employable.

Which best describes you? If you're a passive-dependent person, side-road wanderer or one of the walking wounded, here are a few excuses to hold you over until you decide what you want. The next time Aunt Mary asks, "So you graduated from college, deary. Now what?" Tell her:

1) "I'm going to further my studies in nuclearphysioendoloponium research." She'll be too intimidated to ask more questions.

2) "I'm designing surgical gloves." She'll be too bored to pursue details. Besides, it's all she needs to hear, to be able to tell her friends, you're in medicine.

3) "I'm smuggling contraband." Well...don't expect a graduation gift from her.

Hopefully, once you've finished *Life After College*, you'll have a sharp focus on what you want and you'll be able to move decisively in the direction you've chosen.

WHAT DO YOU WANT TO BE WHEN YOU GROW UP?

ON GOALS

"Once he makes up his mind he's full of indecision."
— Oscar Levant

Although it wasn't written with college graduates in mind, there's a Joe Jackson song that sums up the graduation dilemma perfectly: "You Can't Get What You Want, Till You Know What You Want."[2] Isn't that the truth? There you are, diploma in hand, ready to take on the world, if only you knew what chunk of it you desired.

Or maybe you're one of the "luckier" graduates who looks at this song title smugly. "Of course, you have to know what you want before you can attain it," you say. "And I know exactly what it is." But how can you be sure the direction you're headed in is right? Whether you've based your decision on expert advice, written research, or gut feelings ...the fact remains that most of your life has been spent in school. Since you have limited real world experience, anything you choose is based strictly on an educated guess. "I like studying law," you think. But the decision you've made to become a lawyer doesn't guarantee you'll love the practice. "I always enjoy playing the piano," you say. But will it be as pleasurable to teach? The idea of traveling abroad sounds exciting. But will you feel comfortable in a foreign place?

While seeking advice, doing research, and trusting your gut feelings are all very positive and necessary approaches to goal setting, there's no guarantee, at this point in your life, that you've considered or are even aware of all available options and all the factors that influence them.

Of course, unless you're clairvoyant, it's virtually impossible to predict the future and know for certain that one goal is better for you than another. But there are methods to discover the most suitable course of action. When used correctly these methods will almost guarantee you'll avoid a wrong turn.

---

[2] Joe Jackson, "You Can't Get What You Want, Till You Know What You Want" (New York: Irving/Almo Music Publishers, 1984).

[13]

So how can you be sure you've made the right choice? Or how can you even begin to decide? Let's go back to Joe Jackson's hit. The song begins "Sometimes you start feeling so lost and lonely, then you find it's all been in your mind." There's your answer. The solutions to such questions as "Where do I go from here?" and "Have I made the right choice?" all lie within yourself. Rather than looking to the outside world, you must first do a fair amount of self-assessment. This may sound like an endless process but once you start to really look inside you'll find the rewards of self-discovery are worth the effort. This chapter will take you through the process step-by-step.

For some, the conclusions you draw from self-assessment may be exactly as you thought. For others, they may be as surprising as the lesson taught in *The Wizard of Oz.* When the cowardly lion finally met Oz the conversation went something like this:

"But what about my courage?" asked the cowardly lion anxiously.

"You have plenty of courage, I am sure," answered Oz. "All you need is confidence in yourself."[3]

And for the rest, "what next" decisions may take much longer. But at least this book will provide you with a solid guide against which to compare your options.

So what do you do? First, you've got to look deep within yourself to discover the things you desire most: namely your goals. You have to set them in order of importance: that is, your priorities. Then learn the art of decision-making.

Before you can say you want to be an engineer, go to graduate school or make any kind of decision, it's important that you take a long, hard look at the things you value most. I'm not saying a person can't do something successfully without knowing his or her goals. But if you're aware of your values and know which are most important, the rest of your life will usually fall into place. With your goals as a solid foundation the future will be something you can take charge of. Cecil B. DeMille said, "The person who makes a success of living is one who sees his goal steadily and aims for it unswervingly." Doesn't that make sense? If I decide education is what I want most and go to graduate school, then why am I envious of my friends who are earning sizable incomes? Perhaps I should re-evaluate my goals.

Right now, all this talk about setting goals, priorities, and making decisions might seem like obvious answers to your dilemma. So you might be feeling you already know what's coming next. But in this chapter you will be presented with some proven methods that will reinforce the decisions you've already made and/or help you formulate new ones. What's even better, these methods will not only help you determine your next step now that you've completed college, they'll also

---

[3] L. Frank Baum, *The Wonderful Wizard of Oz* (1900; rpt. Chicago: Rand McNally & Co., 1956), p. 181.

GOAL CHART

1. Primary Goals	2. Priorities	3. Ways to Obtain (Secondary Goals)	4. Priorities	5. Time Span	6. Starting Time

help you make sound decisions throughout your entire life.

Just because a person has set goals and has decided to strive for certain things doesn't guarantee that he or she will obtain them. What these methods will provide is a system for choosing the best path possible. Also goal-setting will enable you to recognize and act upon an opportunity that comes up, either because you've planned it or because a twist of fate has made an unexpected opportunity available.

WHAT'S YOUR PLAN?

"Make no little plans; they have no magic to stir men's blood...
Make big plans, aim high in hope and work."
—Daniel H. Burman

It's time for a little audience participation. If you're reading in a room filled with distractions — vacuum going, dog barking, Bruce Springsteen blaring in the background — then try to escape to a quieter part of your home. You'll need to get yourself as relaxed as possible without falling asleep — so that your mind can be free to wander.

Once you've found a quiet niche, think about the things you value most. Okay, so it sounds corny. But if you take your time and complete the chart on page 15 honestly, you'll learn a bit more about the most important person in your life: You!

For some of you, ideas will come rapidly. In fact, you may even become disturbed that only seven spaces are provided. But if you're anything like I was at your age, you'll be glad there are only seven spaces, not ten.

Now, in column 2, number your primary goals in order of priority. If you have equal feelings about some, give them the same numbers. Then next to each, in column 3, jot down specific ways you can obtain these primary goals. These "ways to obtain" become your secondary goals. This may put you on the spot, but see if you can weigh your likes and dislikes to come up with answers.

Let me give you an example. If you've written "education" in the first column, perhaps one of the ways you can achieve this is by taking the French course you've always wanted to take. So you could write "French course" in column 3. You might also be thinking about getting your MBA. Write "MBA" in column 3 under "French course." Since there are many ways to achieve each goal there are more lines available in column 3 than in column 1. Now in column 4 number in order of priority the secondary goals you listed in column 3. Remember you will have equal feelings about some of them, and you will be able to work on some of them simultaneously. Give these the same numbers. Then in column 5 write a realistic time frame whereby you can attain the items written in column 3. For example, the French course may take three months, so you would write "three months" in column 5. Even if

you think you're going to absolutely love the language and are dreaming of becoming fluent, write three months anyway. It's easier if you
take things one step at a time. The MBA, however, may take four
semesters, so you would write "two years" in column 5. Finally, in the
last column, write a time when you think you'll start pursuing each
secondary goal listed in column 3. "I want my MBA but I'd like to wait
until I travel first," you might say. So put a time when, realistically,
you think you'll go back to school.

This chart is really very easy. Remember anything you write can be
changed, so don't feel you're committing yourself. Just try to complete
it as best you can. If you find you have to leave some things blank, do
so. The whole purpose of this exercise is to get you thinking about what
you want from life.

If I were to fill out the chart according to the example above, it
would look like this:

GOAL CHART

1. Primary Goals	2. Priorities	3. Ways to Obtain (Secondary Goals)	4. Priorities	5. Time Span	6. Starting Time
Education	*1*	*French Course*	*2*	*3 months*	*Spring '88*
		MBA	*1*	*2 years*	*Fall '87*
	2				
	3				
	4				

In a sense you've just been taken. But with good intentions. This
chapter is designed to help you determine what your next step will be
now that you're a graduate. That starts with establishing your goals
and then with setting priorities. Most books would have handled this
issue by first talking about goals and how to establish them, and then
by having you complete a similar chart where you set your own goals.
This book is different. First you'll be filling out a chart according to
what you already know about yourself and your goals. You'll then be
guided through a step-by-step process of analyzing your goals. By the
end of the chapter you'll complete the same goal chart again. The
comparison between the two charts will help you feel more confident
about your decisions — either because your goals remained the same or
because they, in fact, changed somewhat. So let's talk goals.

SOME BACKGROUND ON GOALS

*"It's not enough to be busy...The question is: What are we
busy about?"*   — Henry David Thoreau

Before you can decide what your goals are, you must first have a clear
understanding of what a goal is. *Webster's New Universal Unabridged
Dictionary* says that a goal is "the end which a person aims to reach or
accomplish."[4] It is the final point we strive for. One that will bring
about a desired result.

These desired results are often the same for many people. Happiness,
for instance, is a goal that is universal. Whether a person is young or
old, rich or poor, city dweller or suburbanite, most prefer to be happy.
As a matter of fact, in a survey performed in colleges specifically for this
book, five out of eight students answered the question, "What do you
want most from life?" by saying, "Happiness."

Naturally not everyone strives for the same goals. And even those
that do share common goals don't always approach them in the same
way. For example, happiness means different things to different people.
For some, happiness might be achieved by helping others. They might
reach their goal by becoming volunteers, or maybe health care professionals. For others, happiness may be a very personal achievement
that's obtained through self-enlightenment and spirituality. These individuals might study theology or various methods of self-discovery.

Goals can be long-term. They can be something you strive to attain
all your life—or strive to maintain all your life. Ron is a good example
of both these points. At an early age Ron decided he would need a
sizable income to lead a comfortable lifestyle and provide important
extras for the family he would eventually have. He learned the direct
mail business, recognized its potential and started a company of his
own. It took many years for Ron to build a successful business. But his
hard work paid off. Now he and his family are financially sound.

Ron is a fortunate man. He set a goal, achieved it at a fairly young
age, and works very hard to maintain it.

Goals can be short-term. These goals are usually much easier to
achieve and usually give us a quick feeling of satisfaction. Every time
Karen decides to clean her apartment, no matter how filthy it is, her
feeling of accomplishment usually lasts until the apartment gets messy
again. And for Karen that's a lot quicker than for most people.

The time frame that makes a long-term goal long and a short-term
goal short is really a matter of personal opinion. Take the apartment
cleaning example. Some may consider it a long-range goal. Perhaps
house cleaning is something they do monthly, annually or bicenten-
nially. To them it is a goal unto itself, done every once in a while. But

---

[4] *Webster's New Universal Unabridged Dictionary*, 2nd ed. (New York: New
World Dictionaries/Simon & Schuster, 1979), p. 782.

lor Karen it is done quite often, and she uses it as a stepping stone to one of her longer-range goals: order. This is normally how people manipulate the shorter goals. They use them as steps toward their longer-range desires.

Goals can be general. "I want power," you say. But how are you going to achieve it? When do you plan on attaining power? Is power a real goal or something you sit head-in-hand and dream about?

Better yet, goals can be specific, like the ones a Syracuse University student has. He told me, "My goal in life is to marry a tall Jewish blonde and drive a red Corvette." Now there's a man who knows what he wants! I laughed when I first heard his answer. But think about it. The more specific the goal, the more direct your actions can be to achieve it. For this student, there's no question about what he'll strive for when he graduates. He just has to decide how to meet the woman he wants and how to get the money to buy the car.

There is, of course, another way to look at his presently very specific goals. A wish for something as particular as a tall, Jewish blonde and a red Corvette may actually be two short-term goals that will bring about one long-term desire: namely self esteem. This is basically the way the process works charted on page 15.

So, in summary, it helps to think in terms of two types of goals. First, there are broad categories of primary goals that might be called long-term desires, such as happiness for instance. A goal such as this hardly changes throughout a person's life. What can change are the methods a person uses to attain it. These methods are called secondary goals. They are simply ways to obtain your primary desires. Usually more than one secondary goal is needed to achieve a primary one. And usually they change throughout a person's life.

Here's a short list of goals you might consider primary:

success	wisdom	happiness
prestige	freedom	spirituality
wealth	power	equality
fame	health	order
integrity	love	sensitivity

Which do you value most? How can you work to achieve them? These are issues the next few pages will cover.

Goals come in many shapes and sizes. They are as grand as universal peace and as insignificant as your next holiday outfit. They are as long-term as prestige and as short-term as reading a book. They can be shared, extremely personal, vague or unquestionably focused. Whichever the case, goals are an important phenomenon that can mean the difference between a life that has direction and one that is haphazard.

WHY HAVE GOALS?

*"It's important to make plans, even if we decide to change them,
so that at least for the moment we know where we're going and
we have a sense of progress..."*

— Leon Tec, M.D.

If you were to take a good, hard look at all the successful people you know (and by successful I mean accomplished in one or more of the following goals — happiness, love, wealth) you'd notice outstanding traits they all have in common. They're most likely decisive, self-motivated, and have a sharp focus on specific goals.

All three traits are important; however, the ability to focus on a specific goal may ultimately be the key to their success. Although the first two traits are crucial to each person's progress, without a clear objective to strive for, his or her decisiveness and self-motivation would have been spent haphazardly. Without concrete direction each of these people would have had a hard time forging ahead. But the fact that each put his talents toward a desired result has helped to make them what they are today: successful.

The same can be true for you. If you have a clear understanding of what you value most, your life will be more rewarding. As you move from one stage to the next, you will have a clear perspective from which to make decisions and solve problems. Instead of wandering from college to a meaningless job, you can make a deliberate move, based on your goals, that will lead you closer to those goals. There are times, however, when the decisions we make steer us away from the things we want. But if we constantly review where we want to go and what we want to do, we can get ourselves back on track. After working four years in advertising I finally realized my goals weren't being fulfilled. So I left my job, began free-lance writing and I'm now aiming more directly toward my goal.

Maybe at this point in your life, you feel goal-setting is something you can figure out next year or three years from now. After all, you're still young and probably are responsible only for yourself. Or maybe you feel safe as long as you're taking positive steps, like going to work or school. But as you get older (which, by the way, seems to accelerate with time) you might discover that, without goals, the consequences, of what you've chosen subliminally, have snowballed into something that isn't for you.

For instance, when Janice graduated from college she decided to take a bookkeeping job a friend offered her. It was conveniently located, saved her the trouble of sending résumés and offered her a chance to learn more about accounting from upper management. Janice worked as a bookkeeper for one year; was promoted to the payroll department for two years; then moved on to one of the bigger accounting firms for the next three years. Although Janice is very good at what she does, she's still waiting to get to a level in her career she'll enjoy. She could always look for something else. But she's now earning over $30,000 a year. If Janice starts anything new, she can expect at least a $10,000 drop in salary. For her, this would be a hardship.

Janice's work experience is a good example of why goals should be set early. If her primary motive was happiness, there's no way she would have lasted this long in an unfulfilling career. If her foremost goal was money, then perhaps Janice would ignore her lack of interest and keep plugging along. If continuing in the job was something she'd find impossible to do, then it would be time for her to re-evaluate her plans.

Do you ever find yourself making statements to this effect? "If God had wanted me to be successful, I would have been," or "If it weren't for luck I'd never be able to pay for school." Many of us are guilty of statements like this, implying that we have no control over our lives. To some degree that's true. Just because you've set your mind on something doesn't mean you'll get it. Life is filled with many unexpected occurrences — some good, some bad. That's why it's especially important to know your values. So when life plays its tricks on us we'll be able to avoid a wrong turn or take advantage of an opportunity. The late movie star, James Cagney, considered his fame a matter of luck: "I heard they were hiring actors for a show, and I turned up at the audition hall along with dozens of other would-be's. After a while a man came out — I later learned it was George Kelly, the playwright. He looked over the big crowd, spotted me and said 'O.K., you. You've got the job.' "[5]

But what Cagney failed to say is that it took more than a lucky break to make him a star. If he had had no acting ability, the public would have shortened his career considerably. By knowing his goals and developing his skills in advance, Cagney was able to capitalize on his lucky break.

One way to arm yourself, for both the good and the bad opportunities life brings, is by having a clear understanding of what you want. If you do, then regardless of whether opportunities or misfortunes arise, you'll be able to recognize them as such and take appropriate action.

Patty loved studying to become a nurse, but after three years of emergency room work, she hated to even tell anyone she was a nurse. It wasn't that she didn't enjoy helping people; it was the orders she had to take from higher-ups, plus the shifts she had to work. Patty considered a job at another hospital, but the idea made her even more unhappy. It was time for her to re-evaluate her goals. After a lot of soul-searching Patty decided her happiness was most important. Helping people was next. So she went job hunting. It took several months, but she found a job at a lawyer's office that handled medical suits.

---

[5] Auren Uris and John Tarrant, *op. cit.*, p. 70.

Apparently, her employer was looking for a health-care professional who could investigate medical cases. Patty is living her goals. She's helping people, working nine-to-five, and her boss...well, she couldn't have found a better one.

So you see, not only is setting goals an important process, but setting them at an early age is important too.

WHAT'S FIRST?

"Have a time and place for everything, and do everything in its time and place, and you will not only accomplish more, but have more leisure than those who are always hurrying as if vainly attempting to overtake time that has been lost."
—Tyron Edwards

In his book *Without Feathers*, Woody Allen introduces selections from his private journal in this way: "Following are excerpts from the hitherto secret private journal of Woody Allen, which will be published posthumously or after his death, whichever comes first."[6]

Without Feathers opens with a pretty comical priority, one that fortunately neither Allen nor his publisher stuck by. Nine times out of ten, however, when priorities are observed, they're instrumental in helping us achieve our goals.

Since it's virtually impossible to work on all your goals simultaneously, priorities provide a clear view of how to use your time most effectively. By categorizing goals in their order of importance, you'll have a reference from which to determine when to work on each step and how much time to spend. Of course, there are no hard or fast rules about how long you should stick with each and when to move on to the next, but if you fix a comfortable and realistic limit for yourself, you'll avoid wasting time. Be sure to allot time realistically, since it is defeating to feel you haven't accomplished all you set out to do.

There are instances, however, when you can work on two or more goals simultaneously. If this is the case, it's a good idea to take advantage of the head start. Sharon's plan was to go to graduate school at night, while working all day. She procrastinated for years, thinking a time would arise when working on both her career and degree would be more convenient. This is a classic story. She married, is pregnant, but still wants her MBA. Luckily Sharon and her husband can afford for her to leave work and study full-time. Unfortunately, though, she won't be able to get the degree before "junior" arrives. What started out as an opportunity for Sharon to work on both goals—career and school—ended in her having to make a decision to eliminate one. Although Sharon hadn't taken advantage of her extra time, she did have a good sense of what her priorities were. When she realized work,

---

[6] Woody Allen, *Without Feathers* (New York: Random House, 1975), p. 3.

school and raising a family were impossible all at the same time, she left work to concentrate on school and family. Not everyone will be as fortunate as Sharon to make this transition without thinking about money. So it's important to use your energy wisely, by having a good view of your priorities, and by having the foresight to plan for the unexpected.

Even when you're working on two or more goals at once, there will come a time when one goal must take precedence. If your priorities are constantly reviewed and kept in front of you, you'll be able to shift your focus without hesitation. Just remind yourself what you want and where you're going. This will help you decide which priority should receive the most attention.

Often short-term or secondary goals make us lose sight of our long-term (primary) goals. Reviewing priorities helps you keep tabs on which are which. As long as your short-term plans are contributing to the primary ones, there's no need to worry. Nor do you have to be concerned if your short-term plans are ends in themselves and bring instant gratification. It's when your secondary objectives interfere with primary ones that you should review your situation. Joseph's primary concern was to move up the corporate ladder. When he met Alice, he began to lose sight of this goal. He missed work to be with her and kept late hours. It wasn't until his supervisor complained, that Joseph decided to get himself back on track.

If we could manage having just one goal or main value, we'd have no need for setting priorities. But the fact that we have more than one dream often causes a conflict. With priorities well thought out and constantly evaluated, your conscious decisions (and even your subconscious motivations) will work in your best interest. My first full-time job after graduation was working for one of the major tabloid newspapers — you know, one of those you see on the rack while you're waiting in line at the supermarket. The job allowed me to learn more about publishing, provided some interesting party conversation and, best of all, gave me a chance to write. But I started to realize that my thinking became affected by the stories the tabloid published. So I decided to look for another job. I managed to put off job hunting until the day a woman called me to tell me her dog could talk. When I asked her to put him on the phone, I saw how much the job was affecting me. It was then that I seriously began to look for work. A month or two later, I was offered a position at a filmstrip company. The job gave me more opportunity to write and restored my "sanity." By using the tabloid as a stepping stone and by recognizing the point where it was starting to hold me back from achieving more long-term goals, I was able to resolve my conflict and move to a more rewarding field.

Determining priorities is much like determining goals. Actually, it's easier. It's the step you take after you know what you want. Determining priorities is simply a question of what you want more considering both your needs and desires. So it's not surprising that priorities often change throughout a person's life. In fact, priorities often change throughout society. In 1984 a survey was done by the Gallup organization for *Success Magazine*. It determined that the "idea of success" has changed from materialism to self-enrichment.

"Slowly, during the last 10 years or so, the American concept of personal success has undergone a reversal," the magazine reported. "Old symbols of success—like money, large homes and luxury automobiles—have slipped to the bottom of the list.

"The new criteria for personal success have become the more intangible factors like health, enjoyable job, family, education and good friends."[7]

It's interesting to see how society's values have changed. This doesn't mean that everyone feels this way, of course, so please don't let this observation influence what you feel is best for you. Priorities are a personal decision based on your needs and wants and, if followed closely, can help you achieve your goals.

OBSTACLES THAT CAN AFFECT GOALS

"If there is no wind, row."
— Latin Proverb

This section explains a number of personal, environmental and philosophical obstacles that most of us face at one time or another. These obstacles can certainly affect any honest attempt at goal setting. So it's a good idea to think about your goals while reading the following.

Let's take a look at the personal obstacles that can limit your goals. First, do you regard yourself with proper esteem? Do you have enough self-respect?

Self-respect is a funny thing: somehow it's contagious. If you show others you are confident and worthwhile, they get the same idea. But seeing ourselves as worthwhile and being confident is sometimes very difficult, especially at an age that psychologists label "identity crisis" years. It's bad enough that we're on the brink of many major decisions, but we add to our frustration subconsciously with feelings of inferiority, inhibition and shyness. These feelings are totally normal and to be expected. But are they painful! How many times will you review the conversation you had with Jim, weighing every word and worrying if he still likes you? How many times will you practice what you're going to say or how you're going to act?

These are common concerns we often torture ourselves with as we work slowly to discover who we are. These insecurities are very difficult

---

[7] Susan B. Garland, "How Baby Boomers Are Changing Our Work Ethic," *Gannett Westchester Newspapers*, White Plains, New York, 14 Oct. 1984, p. 4, cols. 1–4.

to deal with and even harder to overcome. What may help, though, is to know that almost everyone has these feelings as they adjust from adolescence to adulthood. More importantly, almost everyone outgrows them. If you're struggling with lack of self-confidence, why not get some help? There are many books available on the subject and many professionals who offer guidance. Be aware that as we become more and more involved in our goals, and as we recognize what's really important in life (and that's a personal discovery), questions of "Am I worthwhile?" subside.

Being afraid of failure is probably the most appropriate issue to discuss next. Life can be humdrum if a person doesn't take chances — educated chances, that is. Life is as exciting as you make it. Likewise, your goals are only as good as you make them. Taking intelligent risks can keep you young and make you interesting. That is not to say that you should rush off to Vegas and put your life savings on the roulette table. But, if you want to travel for a while, switch jobs, move closer to the equator, go for it! Just promise to read the chapter on decision-making first to assure yourself that all the pros and cons have been weighed.

Fear of failure has caused many a person to dig a large rut and lie in it. If you keep in mind that everyone makes mistakes, then making an occasional error will be less threatening. If things don't go according to your plans, there's always something to learn.

Another thing to keep in mind is the old adage "We're each our own worst critic." Life has enough disappointments without our creating more. So be firm with yourself if it's necessary, but give yourself a break once in a while, too.

Of course, maybe it's not you that you're afraid of disappointing. This is something to look at whether you think it applies to you or not. Attempting to fulfill someone else's expectations of you is not always a deliberate action. In fact, most of the time it's a subconscious motive which would require intense self-exploration to determine. However, such self-exploration is usually worth the effort. Make a serious effort to decide whose dreams you are living: yours or someone else's.

At this stage of life, if you're afraid of disappointing someone else, that someone else is usually a parent. This can be a very sticky situation. If you're afraid of disappointing your parents, yet all of you agree on your goals, then your situation isn't so bad. Learning from your mistakes can alleviate a failure if it does occur. But if your parents have different ideas about the direction your life should take, there can be more serious problems. Hopefully these problems can be worked out through discussion, love and understanding. Remind them that a goal is personal. It's something only you can decide for yourself. Be willing to accept advice, but only you can make the final decision, since only you can live your life.

Here comes a twist. Some people actually fear success as if they don't deserve its rewards. These are people who are terrific at self-punishment. Certainly we all experience some self-denial, but fearing success is much more drastic. Consider whether you have this fear as you decide your goals. Are you, in fact, limiting yourself too much? Do your goals stop you from fulfilling your *real* dreams? Do they use your talents to their maximum? These are important questions to ask yourself now and throughout your life.

Also consider whether these are goals you think you *should* or *have to* accomplish. If you're feeling the pressure of an inner policeman telling you "You have to go to graduate school," or "You should look for a job," then beware. If you're taking a course of action simply because that's the way you've always seen it done or always thought it should be done, stop. Look at yourself and determine what it is you really want. Maybe this is a chance to use your own creativity. After all, there are many ways to slice an apple. If there was one way to gain success, happiness, fame, etc., we'd all be doing the same thing. But there isn't. So watch for things you think you *should do* or *have to do*. If they are part of your makeup, let them lead you to something challenging that you'll enjoy.

Celine graduated from college with a BA in education. She taught for a few years, but wasn't happy. No matter how she tried, she disliked teaching. She thought about doing some other type of work but felt obligated to her profession since she'd spent so much time and money studying to become a teacher. Celine kept reminding herself that everything we learn is useful. The more she looked for jobs the more she realized that her degree fit in beautifully with many other fields. So Celine began working in a personnel agency. Today she's much happier with the type of work she's doing.

Maybe you lack encouragement from your friends or family. This can be very debilitating, especially since indecision is always helped by moral support. If parents or friends don't encourage you, then maybe they don't agree with the path you've chosen. If they're pushing you in another direction or rejecting you, then talk to them. Listen to what they have to say. Tell them how you feel. With understanding and communication you're sure to work things out.

Or maybe you're looking to the wrong sources for support. People who aren't interested, or who are too selfish to think of you, aren't going to be encouraging. As you get closer to graduation you will discover, or you may already have discovered, that some of the people you thought were confidants are, in fact, only interested in themselves. It's a typical self-preservation trick on campuses as people start to panic about life after college. At the end of a discussion about goals, you'll suddenly find you've just spent hours listening to a friend's plans and were never given a chance to talk about your own. This is a very common experience. It only proves that everyone is just as concerned about the same things.

As you assume more responsibility for yourself, you will become less dependent on what other people think. You will become stronger in your opinions and much more self-confident. Taking responsibility for yourself will increase self-motivation and help you to establish goals, as well as achieve them.

A final point: It doesn't matter how eager you are to graduate; the real world can make you feel a little lost and lonely. Whether you lived at school or commuted, expect to encounter some social obstacles. It's not easy to say goodbye to your cushioned environment filled with parties, fun, communal spirit. It's even harder to suddenly find yourself thrust into a new environment. For the boarder moving from campus back home, it's life under "their" roof once again. Be prepared for several lectures on the hours you keep, the friends you have, the plans you should be making. Or if you're getting a place of your own, be ready for bills, budgets, an unfamiliar locale. If the world starts to feel foreign, relax. You'll adapt or, better yet, create a niche of your own. Don't be upset that no one is rooting for you to make that touchdown, or that your former RA isn't available for advice. With a little time, you'll adjust. Before you know it, you'll look back on those days with a smile and welcome the new world with enthusiasm. You'll want to work on your goals and will be excited about achieving them.

The next group of obstacles that can affect the goals you set are the environmental kind. These are practical problems that you must consider as you determine what you want from life. The following will help you to gain a more realistic view of your goals, especially those that are secondary.

The first of these environmental obstacles is economic. There are many people who set goals that are financially unfeasible. For instance, graduate school may be on your list, but is it affordable? If not, can you get a loan? Can you work while going to school? Can someone else pay for it? These are very specific questions, but they are good examples of the types of issues you should examine in relation to your goals. Remind yourself frequently that if you want something badly enough, there is, more often than not, at least one way to get it. If you're reviewing your goals and don't think something is feasible, perhaps you should put it off for a while until you can work out the details.

Another factor to investigate is the job market. If your goal is to study to become X or work to become Y—then ask yourself a battery of questions such as: Is the market flooded with my profession? Will the pay be what I'm expecting? Is society changing in such a way that X or Y will become obsolete?

Then, of course, there are always geographical considerations like whether or not the region you live in hinders you in any way. Here are questions you might ask yourself: If my goal is to find happiness by working the land, then what am I doing in Manhattan? If I want to get into advertising, why have I returned to Kansas? If I'm eager to work overseas, then why did I accept a job in Chicago?

What about the media? It affects each and every one of us. Day after day, we are bombarded by advertisements, movies, television and newspapers. Each gives us another view on something that may or may not even be true. Take soap operas. All you'd need is a full day watching them to see how distorted is the life they present. Not only is Christine having Doug's baby and telling Steve it's his, but Heather is embezzling money from Steve so that Christine will leave her poor destitute husband and marry George. After all, George can't turn his back on his son's newborn.

But you don't have to go to these extremes to be affected. How many times have you hummed the McDonald's commercial, dreamt of Christie Brinkley (or Mel Gibson) or thought life would be different driving a Mercedes. Let's not forget the Syracuse student who's anxious to get the red Corvette. And why red? Has some other factor influenced him?

Finally, environmental obstacles also encompass social mores. Questions such as: If all I want is more and more money, where do my values fit in? If your goals and values conflict with those of society, you must be willing to pay the consequences. Gloria Steinem, the world renowned feminist, took a lot of abuse before people stopped to listen. In fact, all the real trail blazers in this world had, at one time or another, to consider their goals in relation to how the public would accept them. It takes a lot of stamina and even more self-confidence to go ahead with your plans knowing the rugged road that can lie ahead.

Let's not forget philosophical issues that affect goals. If you're anything like I was, these can be the most frustrating. After all, is there ever a definitive answer to a philosophical question? One of the biggies that plagued me is, "What's life all about?" For years I tossed this question around hoping to find the answer. And I gave it priority because I figured the answer to this question would be the answer to all my goal-oriented questions. True, it would have been. But there isn't one universally accepted explanation for what life's all about. If this is one issue that torments you, too, then maybe you can come to terms with it by telling yourself life is what you make it. You can then wrestle with the question, "What should I make of my life?"

Then there is the time dilemma. Your questions might be: If I focus on one goal, will there be time to pursue others? Can I do everything? Why does everything take time? This one drove me crazy for a while. I guess its impact started to subside when I became a little lazier. Which, by the way, is something else you can question. Is life to be enjoyed?

Let's not forget the immortality issue! Do I want to leave a mark? If so, how? And here comes time again. If I want to leave my mark will I have enough time?

Philosophical questions are endless. They vary from person to person, as well as from moment to moment. In fact, philosophical questions are certainly something to philosophize about. If these are dilemmas that constantly bug you, maybe you should consider devoting your life to philosophy. . . or better yet, you can do what I did. Accept the fact that you will be eternally plagued by philosophical questions and go about your business.

Whatever that business is, make sure you look at it in relation to those personal, environmental and philosophical obstacles just mentioned, as well as any others you can invent. If your goals reflect any of the implications of these, then it's time for a little revision. If not, then congratulations, you've made some good plans.

By the way, the issues in this section often interfere with our ability to make decisions. So please keep them in mind as you read the chapter on decision-making.

HOW TO DETERMINE GOALS

"First you say to yourself what you would be: and then do what you have to do."

— Epictetus

Establishing goals can sound a lot more intimidating than it really is. If you had a relatively easy time filling in the goal chart, I'm sure you'll agree. For the rest of you, however, it may seem like the moment of truth. But the issue isn't whether or not your goals were easy to articulate. The issue is whether you can discover those goals — because practically everyone has goals at some level of consciousness. Goals are one of those strange phenomena that have been forming within us throughout our lives. Since the time we could think and reason, they have been a direct result of everything we've learned, experienced and imagined. At times, goals lie smack in front of us providing obvious direction. At other times, they lie deep within our subconscious secretly influencing our decisions. If your goals are subconscious it's necessary to bring them to the foreground in order to plan for their fulfillment. One way to do this is by attempting some serious self-analysis.

They say each of us is three people: the person you see yourself as, the person others see you as, and the person you actually are. I can still remember the surprise of having my philosophy teacher call me aside to suggest I study the subject more intently. Up until that day philosophy had simply been a course I was required to take. It was interesting and enjoyable but next semester I would study something else. The professor, however, viewed my performance in his class differently. With his encouragement, I realized that philosophy was a discipline for me and one that was very much a part of my life.

Pitting your opinions of yourself against the opinions someone else has of you is one way toward self-discovery. Often what others think can open new doors to understanding your make-up. If you're honest with yourself, objective viewpoints can add insight. They can help you see yourself more clearly. But remember; an outsider's opinion is helpful only if you're able to look at it honestly while comparing it with your own opinion. Likewise, a person's assessment may be sincere, and our evaluation may be sincere, but they may not be correct. We have to pick apart what's been said while keeping everything in perspective.

Collecting information on how others see you and comparing it with how you see yourself is one way to learn more about what makes you tick. This technique of weighing one opinion against another opinion is better if the advice you're considering is offered spontaneously. Rather than probing good friends about what they think is best for you, listen to the observations and criticisms they make under everyday circumstances. The next time John or Judy tells you to stop complaining about the course you're studying, maybe you should take a look inside.

This technique can also be done retrospectively. But if you do so, be very careful. Taking comments out of context can change their meaning entirely.

Another way to come to terms with your goals is to find a quiet niche where you can relax and let your thoughts run free. Think about what's happened throughout your life. Look carefully at the events, people and things that made you happiest, caused the most grief or provided a feeling of contentment or comfort. Think about the places you've been. The people who influenced you, including the ones you wanted to get closer to and the ones you wanted to withdraw from. Consider what you would change. Look at the material possessions you had, were envious of and now enjoy. Think of your creativity, spirituality and personal growth. Think of what you feel, what you've been taught and what you've developed. Do some free association. Meditate. Fantasize. What are your skills? Hobbies? Achievements? What makes you feel worthwhile? Happy? Excited? Consider your needs, wants and desires. Think of them in relation to you only. Be selfish, very selfish. This exercise is to help you determine your goals and no one else's.

Read the suggestions in the preceding paragraph once more. As you go through them phrase by phrase, write down all the important thoughts you have on each. By giving yourself plenty of time you should be able to compile a pretty healthy list. Now study what you've written, your likes, dislikes, skills and hobbies. Then give the goal chart on page 15 another shot.

Instructions: Most likely you'll handle this chart a little differently than the preceding one. In fact, there are two charts provided this time instead of one. The first is a one-year chart which should reflect the goals you want to accomplish over the next year. The other is a three-year chart which should reflect the goals you want to accomplish after next year.

On the first chart use column 1 to write the goals you value most. You might want to refer to the broad categories of goals listed on page 19. Next to each, in column 2, number them in order of priority. Then in column 3 write specific ways you can attain them over the next year — these become your secondary goals. In column 4 put your secondary goals in order of importance. Then in column 5, determine a realistic time frame whereby you can attain the goals in column 3. Now use column 6 to give a realistic time when you think you'll begin each. After you've completed this chart, take some time and try the three-year chart. Follow the same instructions you've used for the one-year plan.

Hopefully this chart is beginning to look a lot more realistic and much more optimistic. You might want to flip back to page 15 to see what goals you've added, deleted or kept the same. What's changed? Why or why not? If nothing is different, then maybe you haven't been honest with yourself. Or maybe you haven't given yourself enough time. Perhaps you should review again the questions I prompted you with, taking each one a step at a time. Jot down answers to them and notice the pattern that develops. This should help you articulate your goals. For instance, let's say you've always enjoyed music. Throughout grade school and high school you practiced and played the piano. You went through college studying other disciplines, yet still found extra time to include music. Now you've graduated, completed your electrical engineering degree and are eager to get a job. Have you considered incorporating your love for music with engineering? Have you considered a job in the recording industry? This would not only draw upon the obvious skills of music and engineering, but you might find that the long hours that are sometimes required in this industry would be fulfilling, since you are obviously a dedicated and self-disciplined person.

You want to be happy. You're eager to make some money. You don't want to do what everyone else does, but your short-term goals are unclear. By looking at your likes and skills (music and engineering) and matching them with your strong personality traits (self-discipline and dediciation), it will be easier to see how you can set long-term and short-term goals.

Now try this exercise. Make a list of 25 activities you love to do. Whether it's traveling, reading a novel, going to the movies, or studying Latin, write 25 things you like to do most. Then code them as follows:

S — activity done alone
O — activity done with others
L — activity done with a loved one or special person
$ — activity done that requires money
P — activity that requires some planning

Now rank each activity in order of preference. You may want to give some of them the same priority but certainly not all will be equal.

Take some time to study what you've done. Then give the goal chart another try.

WHAT COMES AFTER GOALS?

"If you want your dreams to come true, don't sleep."
—Yiddish Proverb

Hopefully throughout the goal-setting section, you've learned more about yourself and your long and short-term plans. You might have altered your goals slightly, changed the order of your priorities or kept everything just the way you had planned before reading this chapter. Whichever the case, it's important to keep in mind that goal-setting doesn't stop here. In fact, it's a process that should continue throughout your entire life.

As you become more and more aware of what the world is really like, there may be times when you will want to alter your plans slightly or even change them drastically. I saw Jim last year, and he was determined to make it big in advertising. Things seemed to be going well. He had landed an entry-level position with a medium-sized New York agency. The next time I saw him, though, Jim's goals had shifted considerably. After giving it the "ole college try" he had become totally disillusioned with advertising and decided to re-structure his plans. This is nothing new. Within the first few years after college, it's common for graduates to change their direction. First of all, your understanding of things while still in college may vary dramatically from the way you see them after graduation. All of a sudden you find yourself immersed in a whole new world of competition, office politics, taxes, living expenses, prejudices, and the list goes on. The easy road you may be paving to reach your goals can often be interrupted by setbacks that had never entered your mind back in school.

Of course, the positive side of all of this is that something you may be viewing as difficult and unattainable may become more fascinating and more easily achieved. This all depends on your persistence and the circumstances relating to your goals. That's why it's so important to scrutinize your plans and priorities at vital points throughout your life.

In addition, factors such as technological advances, societal changes and economic circumstances may also require you to review and possibly alter your goals. Drema Howard, Associate Director of Career Planning and Placement at the University of Kentucky says, "No longer can we rely on the theory that since X happened in the past, X will happen again in the future. In other words it's necessary to remain flexible in these turbulent times, as well as to follow a good set of goals. Take the job market for instance. In the past few years we have seen many major demographic changes: more senior citizens in part-time jobs, new technologies introduced, and more women in the work force.

These changes can certainly affect a graduate's plans."

So setting goals, especially short-term ones, is a continuous process. From year to year, month to month, maybe even day to day, it's important to review these and remind yourself what you want and where you're going. Look at the priorities you've set and the external factors that influence you. Be aware of your progress. Remember, a goal is only as good as you make it and only attainable if you act upon it. We all know people who say they're planning to do something one day and five years later they're still planning to do it. What are they waiting for? Don't they realize in order to make things happen, *they* have to take action? If five years have passed without them making a move, perhaps they should re-evaluate their goals? Self-motivation is not always easy, and for some it's practically impossible. But unless you take the initiative to achieve your goals, there's no way they will ever become a reality.

Unfortunately, even if we devote a lifetime to achieving goals, it's usually very difficult to attain them all. Some will come easier than others. Some you will devote more time to than others. But there is no guarantee that spending time on something will make it occur. Life's great that way! I'm being sarcastic, of course, but I can alleviate the pessimism by saying if you devote enough time to one plan, chances are you will achieve part, if not all, of that plan...providing it's realistic.

Say you do achieve a goal; then what? Since attaining a goal never provides you with some absolute satisfaction, setting goals is a lifetime process. By picturing each as a stepping stone to some higher place, your life will ideally become a series of successes reaching toward bigger and better accomplishments.

So just when you thought this goal business was taken care of you find it's just begun. Don't let that discourage you. Be thankful that you live in a society where you can plan your future and change it if you want. Besides, working and striving towards a goal or goals is rewarding, enjoyable and exciting in itself.

3.

HEADS OR TAILS?

FACTS ABOUT DECISIONS

In his short story, "The Lady or the Tiger?", Frank Stockton[8] writes about a king who's developed a pretty barbaric method for trying accused criminals. On an appointed day the subject must appear in a public amphitheater to make a decision that will determine whether or not he's guilty. In front of the royal family and hundreds of townspeople, the accused must choose between one of two doors. Behind one is a beautiful, young maiden he'll immediately marry as a reward for his innocence. Behind the other is a ravenous wildcat that'll tear him to shreds as punishment for his guilt. Without any guidance or influence, the subject must make his life or death decision.

Do you ever feel like this? Do you ever make a decision leaving the outcome to chance? Without having a proven method for making a choice, even the most insignificant decision can as life threatening as the one in "The Lady or the Tiger?" You've probably all had experiences when something as small as what to wear or as important as what school to enroll in has made you fret. Then after you've made up your mind you still ask, "Have I done the right thing?" For minor choices this probably doesn't happen all the time. But it can for major decisions. And when it does, your choices can leave you feeling very unprepared and frustrated (not to mention how they can affect your life).

This is usually what happens when someone bases his or her entire decision on a hunch. Putting your stock in a gut feeling is okay if you're on a game show wondering whether to pick the curtain or the box. But I'm sure you'd hate to rely solely on intuition if you were choosing between one job offer or another, one school or another, travel or volunteering.

Feeling frustrated during and after a decision also occurs when your answer is based on logic only. Just as you shouldn't rely solely on

---

[8] Frank R. Stockton, "The Lady or the Tiger?" in *The Lady or the Tiger? and Other Stories* (New York: Scribner, 1884).

intuition, neither can you deny your feelings when making decisions.

Since people are made up of reasoning and emotion, it's important to consider both during the decision-making process. With your logic drawing upon your rational knowledge and your feelings drawing upon instinct and intuition, you'll have a winning combination from which to base a conclusion. For one thing, when both thinking and feeling come into play, you're able to analyze a situation more completely. You'll gather options, evaluate them, and imagine outcomes all by considering what you think and feel, and by considering the way you'll think and feel after you've acted on your choice.

When I began to study the flute, the first thing my instructor taught me was how to breathe. It seemed ridiculous considering I had been breathing for the past nine years. But the same is true for decision-making. Undoubtedly there's a lot more to the process than simply making a choice. What better time than now — the beginning of your life after college — to make sure you have a good method to use.

After all, life is full of decisions. From the time you get up in the morning until the time you sleep, you've made a lot of them. Most of them are trivial: whether to turn on the television or the radio; walk to the post office or get a ride. Other decisions are more monumental: whether to get a job or try for dental school; whether to take yoga or join Nautilus; whether to call your doctor or put it off another week.

It doesn't matter how old you are, what religion you are, what your background is. It doesn't matter what your economic status is or what your personality is like, each of us makes decisions every day and most of them have one common denominator: some degree of unpredictability. The fact that each of us makes decisions means that we all must choose some future course of action based on an unknown result. That's why it's so important that each of us has a decision-making process that helps us make "good" decisions.

It's funny. When we speak of "good" decisions, most of us immediately think of the *result* of a choice, whether or not it brought good fortune. But what actually makes a decision good is the process by which it was determined. Although rash judgments sometimes lead to positive things, the odds are not in your favor. With a good decision-making method, not only will positive results come more often, but the few times that they don't, you'll be better prepared.

Take Glen, for instance. His impulse was to accept the first job he was offered. Instead he did a more thorough decision-making analysis. He went on more interviews, did more research, evaluated his options and then made his decision. Glen still chose the first job he was offered, but he then had a better understanding of why. Unfortunately, after almost a year, Glen was disgusted with his job. He was treated unfairly and was underpaid. But he had in part accomplished what he set out to do. Even though he had hoped to go further with the company, and become a more integral part of the staff, his thorough decision-making practice gave him the foresight to gain as much experience as possible. For Glen this meant better pay and more responsibility at the next job.

The relationship between decision-making and goal-setting is paradoxical. It's like the chicken or the egg riddle. In order to make sound decisions, it's important to have a clear view of your goals and priorities. But in order to form goals and priorities you have to make sound decisions. So if you're still having trouble with the goal chart, this chapter can help. Likewise, if your goal chart is complete, it'll help you make sound decisions from now on.

Remember decisions are not ends. They're steps that lead to some desired point. They continue throughout your life and can become automatic or changeable throughout your life. The choices that are automatic are usually insignificant ones. At one point you made a sound decision that brought a favorable result. So every time the same type of situation occurs, you react routinely. Ever since I missed the bus, I decided to dress before eating breakfast. If I'm running late I can always leave my house without eating, but I refuse to leave my house without being dressed!

Conversely, decisions can be changed. Now that I work in my home, I can eat and dress without worrying about a bus ride. So each morning I make my choice.

Decision-making improves with practice. Not only can insignificant decisions help you make other small choices. They'll also lay the groundwork and confidence to help you come to terms with more pressing problems. And best of all, decision-making will give you control over your life. Rather than rushing into something or avoiding it, you'll face each dilemma with a proven method that works!

Besides, not only is sound decision-making a skill you'll find personally rewarding, but it's one that's marketable too. In a recent *New York Times* article, Daniel Goleman reports on successful executives and the role decision-making plays in their success. "Recent research, for instance, suggests that the most successful corporate leaders think in a style notable for its complexity," according to Dr. Siegreid Streufert, a behavioral scientist at the Pennsylvania State University of Medicine. "This so-called cognitive complexity does not depend on IQ; instead it describes a way of approaching decision-making...

"The successful executives have the mental capacity, the temperament and the inclination to confront complexities even in small problems. They tend to plan long into the future taking into account all possible events that can be anticipated, as well as consequences of these events."[9]

Would you like to know more about the decision-making process? If your answer is "no" you've made a bad decision.

---

[9] Daniel Goleman, "Successful Executives Rely on Own Kind of Intelligence," *The New York Times*, New York, 31 July 1984, p. 1, cols. 1–3.

A FIVE-STEP DECISION-MAKING PROCESS

There are five steps to making sound decisions: the problem; alternatives; evaluation; time and action; re-examination. Let's look at each in detail.

Step 1—The Problem: It would be nice not to have them but problems are a fact of life that start us on the decision-making track. I don't think it's necessary to go into a discussion of what a problem is. We've all had plenty. But I do think it's important to point out that problems can be good, as well as bad. I think when most of us hear the word we cringe—expecting danger to be near. But a problem can be an opportunity, a challenge, as well as a difficulty.

Problems are both conscious and subconscious. I wouldn't dare begin to examine any of the subconscious problems we may have. An expert in psychology is better equipped to handle them. But I can talk about the conscious actions we can take to start the decision process rolling. Probably the best way is to evaluate your life. If you're unhappy, if your needs and desires aren't being met, then you have some choices to make. If you want to try something new or you find your goals have shifted slightly, then it's also time to make some decisions.

Likewise, external factors can put you in a decision-making situation. If there are outside circumstances limiting your needs and goals, if a major change is about to occur (let's not forget graduation), then some serious thinking is in order.

The first thing to do is recognize that a dilemma or challenge exists. At times this is harder than it sounds. We've all been guilty of denying a problem because we don't feel like dealing with it or can't accept the fact that we have it. But in order to make life more fulfilling, in order to make a decision, we must first recognize the problem by being honest with ourselves. "I'm too self-conscious to make that speech." "I don't want to go back to my quiet, little hometown." "I can't decide which job to take." These are some serious problems you may be experiencing as you begin your life after college.

When a problem like this exists you should analyze it to be sure you clearly understand that it is, in fact, the problem. All too often we think we know what our dilemma is, but we never stop to really look at it. If we did we'd be sure to treat the actual problem rather than any peripheral ones.

When Steve was fired from his sales position he refused to believe it was because of his work performance. He kept thinking the reason was a personality conflict with his boss. Once his ego stepped aside, he got a clearer picture of what actually happened. He was fired because he was lazy. He didn't follow up on sales calls, never kept records and was never on time. Only when Steve got to the real problem could he begin to make decisions that could benefit him.

The more you know about your problem, the more specific it is, the easier it will be to put it through each step of the decision-making process. So when an opportunity or difficulty arises, give it some serious thought. Look at it. Be sure it is, in fact, the problem. Be honest with yourself. And accept the challenge with confidence.

Step 2 — Alternatives: You've got your problem clearly defined. Now what? The next stage is to gather solutions, as many as possible along with as much information on each as you can. The number of options you collect will depend on the type of decision you're making. Certainly, some will require more research than others and will take more time to consider. So here's some advice on how to get started.

One way to come up with solutions is to draw on your own resources.

Think about your goals, priorities, needs and use them as a basis for developing choices. Rely on your imagination. Read books and watch shows for background data. Even if an option sounds far-fetched write it down along with the others and include all particulars. You might find it's the best idea you have. Or better yet, it might trigger a list of other ideas. Daydream, meditate and fantasize. This sounds a lot like the goal-setting advice I've given you in chapter 2. In fact, you might want to turn back to page 13. Reading the chapter again may help you conjure up other alternatives.

How about asking an expert? Since people love to give advice and are flattered when asked, talk over your ideas with professionals. Not only will they be able to provide information on the choices you've already accummulated, but chances are they'll be able to supply even more options.

Keep in mind an expert's time is valuable, so it's a good idea to be prepared for your discussion. Having a series of well-thought-out questions will furnish a great start even if the conversation leads you in another direction.

While you're on a roll, why not ask the advice of several professionals? Some people stop after one interview or feel their work is done if they've asked two experts who agree. But the more opinions and facts you get, the better. After all, your decision is only as good as your best alternative.

Asking people who aren't in the area you're considering can also be a great help. Often friends, family, the girl at the pharmacy will bring up an issue or idea you hadn't thought of.

And, don't forget to write for any available information. Keep in mind, however, any brochure you receive is probably a biased advertising piece.

The best way to make a decision is to gather as many options as you can and as much information on each. Of course, it's virtually impossible to glean everything available. That could take a lifetime. But the nature of each decision will determine how much time and effort you should put into it. If the decision is a minor one, collect a comfortable amount of data. If it's monumental, take your time and carefully assemble facts. Keep an open mind and try not to overlook anything.

One more piece of advice: It's better to gather all your options and their pros and cons before evaluating any of them. Some of us have a tendency to start evaluating one before we get all the supporting information. Additional facts may make an option more appealing. Also, an option we may toss aside can be reworked or combined with one we like. This can result in a much better alternative.

Back in his senior year of high school, when Jake was rejected from Yale, he threw out the idea of ever going to an Ivy League school. Even though Yale is an extremely competitive establishment each Ivy League school has its own code for selecting students. Jake might have been accepted at one of the other ones. He certainly had an impressive grade-point average. Or if those other schools rejected him, too, he might've gone to a less competitive school, given himself time to adjust to the college way of life, then tried to transfer. Instead, Jake never explored all his options and enrolled and graduated from a school he was never happy attending.

Step 3 — Evaluating Alternatives: It'll all fall into place. If you have a healthy list of options, good supporting information, the next step — choosing an alternative — will be relatively easy. So why not do a final check?

Look over your material and think about the sources you consulted. If you used printed matter make sure the books, pamphlets, etc. were current. Some decisions can be drastically affected by an outdated piece of information. Be sure the professionals you consulted were reliable. If you feel uncertain about the accuracy of their advice look for back-up facts. Find out their credentials. Ask others about them. And don't assume anything, especially if the decision you're making is an important one. Verify any questionable data and confirm any details you'll rely on heavily.

Once you're content with what you've gathered, thoroughly analyze each alternative by asking these questions:

What risks are involved?

What can I gain?

What can I lose?

What can others gain?

What can others lose?

Is it practical?

What obstacles stand in the way?

Am I being realistic?

Will people approve or disapprove?

Do I approve or disapprove?

Of course, not all these questions will apply to every decision and by no means is this list complete. But it will give you an idea of how to weigh pros and cons. During this time don't forget to consider your feelings as seriously as you consider your logic. Judge each option in relation to how it'll affect and be affected by your long and short-term goals.

I have a friend who made two very important decisions one summer: to marry and to go to law school. The marriage wasn't the choice that upset me. Nor was the decision to go to law school. What worried me was the way she handled her long and short-term plans. Her idea was to get married before she started school so that her studies wouldn't be interrupted by wedding arrangements. This was reasonable. But she chose to attend a no-name law school over a prestigious one so that she could honeymoon a few weeks in Europe. Apparently, classes at the no-name school began three weeks later than the other. Why would anyone opt for a few weeks abroad when it could drastically affect the quality of her education? My friend's priorities are obviously different from mine. I think she made her choice without considering her long-ange goals.

In addition to weighing pros and cons, go through your list and imagine all the possible outcomes of each choice. That includes the good and bad outcomes. An exercise of this sort will help you draw conclusions, in addition to preparing you for any unexpected consequences.

Bill is an expert at this approach. Before he makes a decision he looks at his list of choices and imagines scenarios relating to each. He creates conversations, obstacles and new challenges using every possible combination of events, people and situations that could occur as a result of his decision. Bill was ecstatic when he got accepted into the Air Force flight-training program. But it meant that he would be leaving his family and friends for an extended period. Bill eased the pain for all parties involved by having a pre-ordained notion of how everyone would react and how he'd handle each. When his Mom cried, he showed her his itinerary and wrote down the visits he'd be able to make back home. Conversely, when his friends congratulated him, he was ready to celebrate. Imagining bad outcomes, as well as good, makes Bill a much better decision-maker. He's prepared for disappointments and more attuned to unexpected opportunities.

Like goals, your decisions should be your own. It's good to seek advice but your choices should be tailored to your own needs and wants. Since you come from experiences only you had and since your morals, values, likes and dislikes are what make you who you are, then your decisions should be yours too. Let's look at the last two steps to the process.

Step 4—Time: Remember the Rolling Stones' hit single, "Time Is on My Side"? In the decision-making process you too can put time on your side. By setting deadlines on when to make a decision and determining when to take action, you can manipulate time so that it's used most effectively.

So how much time should you spend on a decision? There are really no hard and fast rules that apply. It varies from decision to decision depending on the importance and the circumstances affecting it. For larger decisions we usually want more time than smaller ones. But it isn't always available. For some New York City cops, serious split-second choices have to be made every day. In life-or-death situations we can be pressured to consider factors under dreadful deadlines. But with most other problems, choices can be settled within a comfortable time frame.

Determine the value of the choice you're making and how it affects your long- and short-range plans, then figure in ample time to collect and evaluate facts. Leave a little extra cushion for surprises, like an option that might come up unexpectedly. This will provide you with a deadline that will help you avoid panic and rash judgments.

Since there's no magic moment when a decision comes to you, a deadline compels you to make a commitment. By imposing your own time frame, you can ease additional stress. Of course, in most instances, deadlines can be extended. But this is a factor you should consider in special cases only. If a person gets into the habit of postponing deadlines, his or her goals can be stunted.

You've made your decision. When do you put it into action? After you've decided what you want to accomplish, the logic of the situation will usually dictate when to take action.

Some of us may find action the toughest step of all. But unless you take responsibility and put your choice into play, then the whole decision-making process is ineffectual.

Since the day I met Kevin he's been unhappy with his roommate. He complains about the dishes his roommate leaves, the creepy friends he has over, the groceries he snitches. Kevin always sums up our conversation with "I've decided to look for another place." But I can guarantee the next time I see him, it'll be "that lousy roommate" story all over again. It's not good enough that Kevin chose to move. He's got to get off his rump and do something about it.

Step 5 — Re-Examination: Here's another similarity between goal-setting and decision-making: the re-examination stage. Since decision-making is a continuous process, too, it's important to do a careful, objective re-examination of the choices you've made so that:

1) you can perfect the results of the decision by working on specific details it involves.

2) you can make better decisions in the future.

No matter how terrific or how horrible the outcome of a decision may be, there's something to be learned. Scrutinizing the gains and losses, as intensely as the steps you took to arrive at your choice, will help you improve your decision and help you make sound judgments.

Since decision-making gets better with the right kind of practice, re-evaluation is imperative. Note what you've learned about yourself in the process. Remind yourself what your goals and priorities are. Consider how the decision affected your future, your friends, family, acquaintances, its impact on you and the amount of time it took to determine.

Not all your decisions will turn out the way you expect, but the odds will be more in your favor as your decision-making skills improve.

Decisions with good outcomes can be made even better. And those with bad results can be changed. It's important to note that changing your mind to make a better choice is not a weakness. It's a positive step. But be careful. Make sure you know exactly why you've made the switch and reconfirm your move by investigating every detail.

Pam was all set to attend a graduate program at Columbia University until she got accepted. The reality of committing herself to classes, books, studies didn't sit well. Pam re-examined her options, did extra research on each, then decided she'd wait a year before going back to school. To most, Pam appeared flippant. But she knew exactly what she was doing and why. For Pam the advantages of waiting a year far surpassed rushing into the program now.

As with any other skill we learn, our decision-making methods may get rusty, there can be setbacks. If you are thoroughly disgusted with the outcome of your choice, maybe you should alter your decision. Be careful not to make blanket statements. Some people adopt "never again" attitudes that can be very damaging. Do an honest analysis of what went wrong. Look at the steps you took and the ones you may have left out. And more importantly, constantly look for ways to improve your decision-making.

A good decision-making method is an invaluable tool you can carry with you throughout your life. It can help solve such insignificant problems as what brand of beer to buy to very important ones like when to switch jobs. As you approach life after college, having a finely tuned process to make choices by, will give you confidence and help pave the way to a happier, more positive life. Here's a chart that sums up the process in a handy format. You may find it necessary to alter it slightly to fit your needs.

Directions for Decision-Making Chart: Once you've determined your specific problem, write it in column 1 labeled "Problem." Underneath, make a self-imposed deadline that will allow you ample time to collect and evaluate facts. Next, take time to gather options and write them in column 2—"Options." Then separate the results of your research on each into column 3—"Pros" and column 4—"Cons." Weigh the advantages and disadvantages by asking yourself the questions on page 44. Consider the outcomes you may experience as a result of each option. Write them in column 5. Figure when you should take action, column 6, and set a date when you'll review the effects of your choice. Put the date in column 7. The above example should help you complete a chart of your own. Keep in mind, the chart isn't one that you'll be able to fill out in one sitting. Instead it will have to be done in stages as you gather facts and options.

The Pros

The Cons

Facts to Consider

Take Action

Date to Re-Examine

The Problem

The Deadline

Option

Option

Option

Option

PART II.

INTRODUCTION

My sister and I have this running joke. It started at a point in my life when I decided to make some major changes. You know, the kind that keep you up all night, start you smoking, and make you totally impossible to live with. So I went to her hoping for guidance. I figured since she was older, it would be second nature for her to give me sound advice. Instead, after I asked her for her opinion, she said, "Diane, you've got to face the music and dance." A lot of good that did! Now whenever a dilemma occurs, we repeat the cliché.

What does this have to do with *Life After College*? You can thank my sister for the next section of the book. If it wasn't for her vague advice, I probably would have ended the book here. Instead, I now realize the true beauty of being explicit, and have taken the book one step further. Now that your goals are set, your priorities are determined and you have a formula for making decisions—Section II will provide you with the music and teach you how to dance your way through each option.

If you're still a little uneasy about attending graduate school, Section II will tell you what to expect and how to approach it. If you definitely want to join the armed forces, the following part will explain the requirements and give you important details. If you want to volunteer part-time and work full-time—Section II will give you the facts you need to attack both the volunteer and work force. Or if you decide to travel now, the information that follows will help you plan your itinerary. Then when you return home, it'll be waiting with research on how you can direct yourself to your next goal. So here's some background music and the lessons you'll need to dance your way to "success."

NOT BORED OF EDUCATION?

Learning is a life-long process. From the time we're born until the moment we die (and maybe even beyond), learning is a day-to-day accumulation of facts and concepts that can be translated into endless rewards.

What you learn can bring personal gains like power, prestige, self-enrichment, self-expression. And what you learn can bring societal gains. It can help you initiate new technologies, enhance existing policies and maintain status quo.

But the speed at which a person learns and reaps his or her rewards is strictly an individual process. Depending on the goals you've set for yourself and the emphasis you place on education, learning can be something you spend hours on each day or minutes each week.

Every time I decide against reading a book, taking a course, watching an educational TV program, I can still hear Sister Mary Lobotomy yelling, "What's the matter dear? Are you afraid you're going to learn something?" There's nothing like a little Catholic school guilt to keep a person motivated.

If you're a motivated learner, you may want to approach education head-on by going directly to graduate school. Or perhaps, you'll want to take a few courses in subjects you find interesting. Then again you might feel the past 16 years is enough right now and want to take some time off.

Whichever the case, this chapter is designed for all types of learners: from the tough self-starters to the laid-back people who occasionally attend an interesting seminar. And it's written so that no matter when you decide to take the initiative to learn, today or five years from tomorrow, you'll know how to get started. After all, even though education may not be at the top of your list right now, it may be there later.

This chapter has been divided into two sections: the first focuses on graduate study; the second on a less-structured education.

GRADUATE STUDY

So 16 years of schooling isn't enough? Are you sure? Many recent graduates make the mistake of plunging into graduate school for the wrong reasons. Unless you have a lot of money to spend, it's a good idea to evaluate and re-evaluate your decision. As discussed in the goal-setting section, consult friends, professors, relatives, alumni, and professionals in your field of interest.

Ask if an advanced, graduate degree is definitely the way to attain your goal. Furthering your education is a great thing as long as you're continuing for the right reasons. Is education your top priority? Will it further your career? Can it bring you closer to your dreams?

Let's look at some of the possible benefits of completing a graduate program:

• In our society it's common to have a bachelor's degree in order to get the better jobs. Taking your education a step further can usually give you an edge over work place competition.

• In many cases, having an advanced degree means a higher starting salary. Of course, there are exceptions, like the woman I worked with some years ago. She had a PhD in philosophy and was having a very difficult time finding a teaching job. Secondary schools claimed she was overqualified, universities had limited openings.

• Since a graduate degree provides you with a sophisticated background in your area of interest, as well as a knowledge of the latest skills and techniques—then having one often enables you to bypass entry level jobs.

• Advanced degrees can also help a member of a minority group, including women, outshine competitors.

• It's often a quicker way to climb the corporate ladder.

• It can enhance a business of your own.

• It can bring many personal rewards: it may improve your lifestyle, increase your self-esteem, extend self-expression, to name a few.

• What's even better, having a graduate degree can help you enrich society. As mentioned before, it's people with expertise that our nation depends upon for new technologies, effective policies, etc. Unfortunately, however, in a recent article by John Brademas, President of NYU, he warns us of the serious shortages of graduate trained experts in the actual sciences. Unless more students attend graduate schools there could be a serious problem in meeting the "nation's imperatives and expectations."[10] In fact, it's through our country's needs, that graduate study was born.

---

[10] John Brademas, "Graduate Education in America," *Vital Speeches of the Day*, 1 Apr. 1984, pp. 374–375.

The Best University For You

Remember the factors that determined the university you attended? They should be the same for selecting a graduate school. Even though your priorities might have shifted slightly, the considerations should basically be the same. I'm not talking about male/female ratio; concerts on campus; athletic team ranking. To select the best school you've got to look at what you want to study in relation to the program the school offers; the university's location; it's reputation; tuition; and requirements. Let's look at each in detail.

University's Program

Graduate programs vary greatly from university to university, department to department. What may be considered a rigid curriculum in one school or one department may be a lot freer in another. For instance, most graduate schools organize their curricula around introductory courses, concentrated areas of study and electives. Some have a fixed curriculum with no electives. While others allow students to personally arrange their whole programs. It's important to consider this factor and how it affects and fulfills your needs and wants before selecting a school.

Likewise, teaching methods are also as individual as a school is, or as a department can be. Some professors offer a concentration on research and written exercises. Others emphasize seminars, while many stress a combination of hands-on experience and oral participation. Which teaching method appeals to you? And which do the schools you're looking at offer?

University Location

Determining the geographical location where you'd like to attend school depends largely on whether you'll be a full or part-time student. If you're a part-time student, chances are you'll want to attend a school that's within a comfortable distance from a career-related job or even a temporary job. After a full day of work you may already feel drained; a long commute will only add to your fatigue. Besides, easy access will give you more time to use school facilities like the library and labs, plus enable you to get in touch more often with faculty and classmates.

Since most students can only afford to be in school part-time more and more universities are making provisions. Many offer classes in early mornings, evenings and weekends. Some even hold lectures during train rides to and from work! This too may be an important reason why you choose one university over another. After all, being a part-time student/full-time employee is often a stressful situation. The more convenient a learning environment is, the less pressure you will feel.

Of course, if there's a terrific program available part-time that isn't easily accessible, perhaps you'll consider relocating. Usually a campus is surrounded by many shops, restaurants, etc. that provide business and residential opportunities.

On the other hand, if you're able to enroll in a program full-time, the neighboring area is usually a less important consideration. One of the few times it does matter is if it's necessary for you to gain experience from what lies outside university doors. It's no wonder that most art students want to study in Manhattan. Not only are there many good programs to choose from, but schools are nearby some of the most prominent galleries in the world.

Will you be happy attending your alma mater? It's common for students to decide to continue their education at the school where they received their bachelors degrees. Many feel less pressure in familiar surroundings where their living accommodations are already set.

Or are you ready for a change? After studying four years at one university, students often want a change of scenery, climate, an opportunity to live in another state. Whether that decision means living close to friends and relatives, or in a location that is similar or completely different than what you're used to, is entirely up to you.

So why not visit the campuses you're planning to attend? And be sure to let the admissions office know you're visiting. This not only shows character and interest, but more often than not, will lead to a guided tour of lecture halls, classrooms, etc.

Reputation

As far as reputation goes, universities are like everything else in life. Some are more highly recognized by the public and educational community than others. Students enrolled in MBA programs, for instance, do better in business having graduated from Ivy League schools or say, Stanford University. But like everything else, the best schools are usually the most competitive and the most expensive. These are two other considerations you should think about realistically when looking for the best graduate school. It's a natural tendency to want the highest quality education but will it be affordable? And will you have the ideal requirements? Both factors are discussed later on.

Within the educational community there are a number of organizations that rate and rank schools. These groups evaluate a university at the universities' request, according to an established set of standards. To be an accredited school, most university departments hire professors who teach a maximum of 12 hours a week; 75% of whom have doctorate degrees. In addition, each school library must meet specific requirements, as does each course offered.

There are six major regional groups that evaluate universities. They are Middle States Association of Colleges and Schools, New England Association of Schools and Colleges, Northwest Association of Schools and Colleges, North Central Association of Colleges and Schools, Southern Association of Colleges and Schools, and Western Association of Schools and Colleges. Most universities are accredited by one or all six groups.

In addition, there are a number of specialized organizations that judge and accredit worthy institutions. There are about 37 fields rated by such groups, including medicine, journalism, business and more. You might want to write for accrediting information on schools that interest you:

Council on Postsecondary Accreditation
One Dupont Circle
Suite 305
Washington, DC 20036
(202) 452-1433

Since the quality of education varies between full and part-time curriculums, be sure to tell them whether you will attend full or part-time. And also state which program interests you.

Tuition.

Certainly any tuition is affordable if you have enough money, but most of us don't have enough. That's why it's important to consider tuition, financial aid and what *you* can swing, when selecting graduate school.

You might already know that depending on the school you choose, the price you pay for room, board, books and fees will vary greatly. The range was estimated at $5,000 to $18,000 a year with prices going up every year.[11]

Keep in mind that the more prestigious the school, the higher the tuition. And rightly so. Professors are usually of a higher caliber and facilities are the most advanced.

If prominent schools are out of your league, research city and state universities. Since all are supported by tax dollars, tuition is a lot less expensive. In fact, even if you go to a state university as a non-resident of that state, tuition may still be cheaper than if you attend a private institution.

Tuition is one area especially, where part-time students may benefit. Often employees with career-oriented jobs have a tuition reimbursement incentive. If an employee can show just cause for getting a degree, a company will sometimes refund all or a percentage of tuition expenses. When Bob realized he'd need an MBA to get ahead, he consulted his supervisor. He illustrated how it would benefit the company, how he'd apply his knowledge to his position and how he could pass the information he learned to other employees. Bob was reimbursed for 50% of his tuition.

Tuition is a lot less harrowing when you consider financial aid. Although some monetary support is based strictly on merit, most is awarded on the basis of need. Federal student aid, for instance, is determined by a simple mathematical equation. It's the difference between your educational cost (including tuition, room, board, books,

---

[11] Sharon Grady, "Education — Financial Aid for Graduate School," *Working Woman,* June 1983, pp. 57–58.

supplies, etc.) and the amount you and/or your family can afford to pay. The remainder is evaluated with such information as family and personal income, assets and benefits. This would be represented on your financial aid application. To find out whether you may be eligible for federal or private financial aid, look at some of the resources listed in appendix A.

Financial aid can be broken into three basic groups. Let's briefly look at each:

Grants/Scholarships. These are usually awarded on the basis of merit, so you can kick yourself now if you goofed-off as an undergraduate. You might even kick yourself harder when I tell you they're not something you have to pay back. To find out which are available at the schools you want to attend, consult the financial aid administrator.

The public library also has information on state and private sources of financial aid. Ask the librarian for assistance. If you think you're eligible, check into foundations, religious groups, town and city organizations. Some organizations offering funds are listed in the U.S. Dept. of Labor's Occupational Outlook Handbook and can be found in the Book of Associations. They are referenced in the bibliography. And don't overlook any employers or labor unions that your family members may work for. They often provide special funds for students like you.

College Work Study Programs. It's learn while you earn! Programs of this sort provide jobs on and off campus for students who need monetary support. A university will designate a certain number of hours each week when you will have to do such tasks as grading undergraduate quizzes, tutoring undergrads, monitoring exams, etc. The university schedules you by taking your work load, health and capacity into account and usually pays current minimum wage. But before you can be considered for such work-study programs, you must, of course, be accepted into a school.

Loans. If all else fails or just isn't enough, you can always borrow money. Many colleges, banks, lending institutions offer special loan terms, interest rates and repayment features for students who need money for educational expenses. The best loan of this type would be one that has low interest rates, no interest charges and one you don't have to repay until after you graduate. So shop around for the best deal since terms will vary from establishment to establishment.

For details on specific loans offered to graduate students, and for sources of further financial information, turn to appendix A.

Requirements.

Past experience probably showed you that some schools demand higher standards from their applicants than others. When you applied to college your school grades and SAT scores were a good indication of the universities that would accept or reject you. In the case of graduate schools, however, not only do the standards vary from university to university, but so do the requirements. Some ask only for an admission application accompanied by transcripts and entrance exam scores — while others ask for these and more: like letters of recommendation and interviews with department heads.

Since it's virtually impossible for this book to provide you with the specific standards and requirements for each graduate school, consult relevant books published by Barron's and Lovejoy. Or better yet, write to the universities that interest you and be sure to address the appropriate department. (Graduate requirements also differ from department to department. It's not enough to write to the admissions office only, especially in a school that offers literally hundreds of graduate programs.)

To give you an idea of what to expect and how to approach graduate school requirements, let's take a closer look.

The Admission Application. Otherwise known as filling out a form, the admission application is fairly easy to complete. (If it's not, then perhaps graduate school isn't for you.) Universities ask pretty basic questions that you should answer clearly, neatly, and succinctly. And some require a written essay on why you'd like to concentrate your studies in a specific area. If the school you're applying to asks for an essay, remember that it's better to write a short concise page than to treat the essay like an exam question you have no idea how to answer. We've all had that harrowing experience of writing page after page about everything except what we were asked. Don't do that here. Be specific, pithy, read it over several times and get opinions!

Of course, don't expect that applying to graduate school is free. Most universities ask for a nominal fee of approximately $25 to process your application. Fees also vary from school to school.

Undergraduate Grade Point Average. Don't start regretting all those nights you crammed for a test rather than scheduling enough time to study. Your grade-point average is only one of several factors taken into consideration when being reviewed for acceptance. In fact, the American University in Washington, DC asks that each applicant answer the following questions when writing their entrance essay: "Do you consider your transcript(s) of college work an accurate indication of your academic ability? If not, why?" If you ask me, that's a very nice opportunity to compensate for low grades if, in fact, you have them. And a question like that certainly shows that university review boards are composed of people who are willing to give you a chance. So don't be upset if your social life sometimes got priority over your school work. Just turn over a new leaf.

Most schools use a mathematical equation to determine your academic standing. They multiply your overall grade point average (GPA) by 200 and add your entrance exam score (discussed later in the chapter). Highly accredited schools normally accept students with a minimum total of 950–1000. Check the schools that interest you to see what they require.

If your GPA looks like it'll affect your chances of being accepted, don't be completely discouraged. After all, some university review boards rely more on other requirements than previous academic status. For instance, universities that want a healthy cross-section of students may give minority group members an extra boost. In some cases, people with military experience have an edge. Applicants who are coming back to school with substantial work-related experience may also have an advantage.

Letters of Recommendation. To get a better idea of the kind of person you are, many schools ask for letters of recommendation. Dr. Turner of Michigan State University says, "The best people to ask for a character reference are those that not only know you well, but have some connection to the field you want to study."

In certain instances a university will supply you with a pre-printed form that asks the people you choose specific questions about you. In other cases, the university will ask a recommender to write an essay that includes information about your previous accomplishments, intellectual independence, ability to work with others, etc.

Whichever type your school requires, be sure to choose people who will give you a good reference. Your decision should be made among people who know you fairly well and who will take the time to complete a form and/or compose a letter that puts you in the best possible light. Choose people who will comply with deadlines and who are aware of your background, accomplishments and goals. Some suggestions include alumni, professors, employers and friends.

Personal Interview. You may consider this "cruel and unusual punishment" but many universities require a personal interview before selecting who will attend. If that is the case with the school you're applying to, remember one important fact: you should be interviewing the university just as eagerly as they are screening you. After all, grad school costs a lot of money. You'd better be getting the most for it.

With this in mind the day you meet with department heads, advisors or both, be prepared with a list of important questions. They should be ones that show you've done research and reveal just how enthusiastic you are to be accepted. Avoid inquiring about basics like information that can be found in university brochures. Instead ask particulars. Be ready to discuss your goals, the steps you've taken to achieve them and the ones you're gearing yourself to accomplish.

An interview of this sort should be considered a professional meeting in every aspect from dress to salutation, to fielding tough questions and asking pertinent ones. In fact, for a good check on whether you'll be prepared, take a look at Appendix K. Although it is written specifically for those going on a job interview the advice definitely relates to an interview of this type too!

Entrance Exams. You didn't think your test taking days were over, did you? Many schools require each applicant to take an entrance exam as part of their evaluation process. These exams vary depending on the discipline you want to study, yet most don't concentrate on specific questions relating to each field. (The medical entrance exam and the subject test of the GRE are exceptions.) Instead, entance exams measure mental skills — like reasoning, reading comprehension and logic — that are an integral part of each discipline. It's no wonder that many people who major in math, for instance, can go on to law school, never having studied political science.

Graduate school entrance exams are much like the SAT's. For starters, they are developed and scored by accredited testing centers, not the universities themselves. And they consist of timed segments, where you read inquiries from a test booklet and answer on a separate sheet with everyone's favorite: the #2 pencil.

Whether you plan to go directly to graduate school or take some time off, it's a good idea to prepare for entrance exams. Not only will you have a clearer view of what to expect, but preparation has been proven to raise a person's score considerably. There are several books written for each test. Your library and local bookstore can help. And so can review courses that are offered. Your university might have such a course.

Not everyone will have to take an entrance exam. You might be relieved to find out the schools you're applying to don't require them. But if you plan on trying for a grant or fellowship then chances are you'll have to take a test. Since monies are given based on merit, most require test scores to determine if you're eligible.

So when do you apply? Much literature suggests applicants take their exams as much as a year in advance. This fact isn't surprising since it will guarantee that schools and fellowship associations will receive your test scores on time. However, some students take their exam as late as one semester before they plan on metriculating.

To learn particulars on each test, the following information will provide testing centers to write for specifics like test dates, fees, registration and sample questions. By the way, testing accommodations are made with you in mind. Tests are administered at hundreds of convenient locations like local universities and colleges. They have provisions for the handicapped. And the tests themselves are easy to register for. In fact, some of you may even go to Ticketron Offices to reserve a seat.

GMAT. The Graduate Management Admission Test helps graduate schools of business evaluate their applicants. This 3½ hour aptitude test consists of eight separately timed sections, each containing 20–35 multiple choice questions, in verbal and math skills. The test is usually given four Saturdays a year in January, March, July and October. For particulars write:

Graduate Management Admission Test
Educational Testing Services
CN 6103
Princeton, NJ 08541-6103
(609) 771-7330

GRE. The Graduate Record Examination is given to students interested in graduate study in any one of a number of areas. It's divided into two parts, a general test and a subject test. This three hour general exam contains verbal, math and analytical ability sections. The GRE is usually administered on Saturdays in February, April, October and December. For more details write to:

Graduate Record Examinations
Educational Testing Services
CN 6000
Princeton, NJ 08541-6000
(609) 771-7670
(415) 849-0950 in Berkeley, CA

LSAT. The Law School Admission Test is administered in approximately 472 US locations and about 62 places abroad. The LSAT is composed of six 35 minute sections that measure your ability to read, understand and reason. One 30 minute writing sample is also asked which is sent and judged by the school you're applying to. For specifics, write or call the following, and be sure to ask for information on the LSDAS (Law School Data Assembly Service) and CRS (Candidate Referral Service). They're services you'll want to consider:

Law School Admission Services
Box 2000
Newtown, PA 18940
(215) 968-1100

MCAT. Otherwise known as the Medical College Admission Test, the MCAT is a six hour exam that tests specific knowledge in fields of biology, chemistry and physics. In addition, it judges analytical skills necessary for the study and practice of medicine. MCAT is given twice a year, in the spring and fall. For more information, write or call:

Memberships and Subscriptions
Association of American Medical Colleges
One Dupont Circle, NW
Washington, DC 20036
(202) 828-0548

That about wraps up graduate study: how to choose a school, the prerequisites involved and some important factors you should consider. Of course, there may be other personal criteria you'll want to base your decision on — like the size of the school, refund policy, drop-out rate

Write to ones that sound intriguing and also to the National Home Study Council at 1601 Eighteenth St., NW, Washington, DC 20009, (202) 234-5100. The council will send you more information on correspondence schools and programs you may have overlooked. What's even better, they'll send information on only the schools they've approved. That means they assure you that each institution has met the following standards:

- has a competent faculty
- offers educationally sound and up-to-date courses
- carefully screens students for admission
- provides satisfactory educational services
- has shown ample student success
- advertises faithfully
- financially able to deliver high-quality educational service.

Of course, there are some home-study schools not accredited by the National Home Study Council. If one catches your eye, be sure to investigate it thoroughly before spending money! Another way to tap educational opportunities in your vicinity is to leaf through local yellow pages under training/technical schools and under specific topics that interest you. The U.S. Department of Education recognizes an organization known as The National Association of Trade and Technical Schools (NATTS). This organization reviews and accredits worthy private residence schools throughout the United States. So if you're thinking about enrolling in a private school contact NATTS at 2251 Wisconsin Ave., NW, Washington, DC 20007, Suite 200, or phone (202) 333-1021. Ask about the institution that interests you, the quality of their courses and the caliber of their faculty.

Don't overlook programs that are given in the evenings at local high schools, churches, clubs and libraries. For information contact the board of education within your area. Go to the library and pick up pamphlets and watch your mailbox. Most local organizations send brochures right to your home! For a listing of seminars and workshops look into the National Directory of Adult Continuing Education, a source compiled by Goodman.

Of course you may have the fortunate experience of being offered the chance to take a training program through the company you work for. Larger companies such as IBM, Bloomingdale's, Citibank and firms like them make educational opportunities available to their employees. If so, here are a few pointers on how to get the most from the course you take:

- Decide what you'd like to get from a course and investigate whether the one you're planning to enroll in will fulfill that need.

and the placement services—so I've listed a number of additional references in Appendix A.

CONTINUING EDUCATION.

The day I graduated from college, there was no bigger relief to me than to know I could go home each night without feeling pressured to cram for three finals or write four term papers. In fact, at times school work was such a burden to me that I think it left me emotionally scarred. It's been eight years since I finished college and sometimes I still dream about waltzing into a class on what I think is the first day of the semester, only to find out it's actually the last one and I have to take the final exam.

If you're a psychology major you'll probably look at this dream as a normal bout with anxiety. But if you're anything like I was the day I finished school then you probably have a less clinical reason why I'd dream something like that. Really wasn't the graduating ceremony more like getting sprung from jail than a commencement exercise?

If you answered "Yes," then welcome to the world of continuing education. It's a place where you can take a few courses, attend an occasional seminar, go to self-help workshops, exercise and learn at home—all on your own time, all without totally committing yourself and all without dreaming of surprise exams.

Adult Education classes can keep you physically fit. With more and more individuals interested in their health, more and more programs are available to keep you in shape. A local listing that came to my home recently advertised everything from ballet and tap to yoga, aerobics and calisthenics.

Taking a workshop or attending a seminar is one way to explore subjects that interest you. For the past 16 years many of the courses you took were requirements for your degree. With the extra time you now have, why not study astrology? Learn to play an instrument? Or dabble in crafts like stained glass, woodworking, quilt-making, watercolors?

Some classes can develop your psyche, like self-hypnosis, meditation and stress management. Others can be used in relation to your career. These are the most in demand, so let's take a closer look.

Taking a few night courses can give you skills that will enhance your performance on the job and help you keep up with technology. Computer courses are now among the most popular offerings. And so are career-boosters like business English, speed reading and typing.

In addition, workshops and seminars are great for people who are switching their careers or who would like to earn extra money. Often residents learn the ins and outs of a new endeavor through courses offered in their community. In my county, real estate classes are always filled to capacity. And certainly classes like furniture upholstery, flower arrangement, auto mechanics and picture framing provide individuals with skills they can have fun with, as well as turn into profit.

Anne certainly made out like a bandit. Two years after she took a calligraphy course, she was hired by several of her sister's friends to hand write their wedding invitations.

And continuing education is terrific for people who want to refresh job-related know-how. It's not unusual for women who have raised a family to take a few courses before returning to the workplace.

Reading books, taking classes, buying educational videos can make you more interesting, keep you in shape or satisfy a curiosity. Continuing to learn can occupy time. (Although at this point in your life you probably don't have to look for things to keep you busy.) It can be pleasurable, develop communication skills and it can help you cope with a problem. There are countless self-help groups springing up every day just as there are countless reasons why a person should learn more about new subjects, from assertiveness training to psychic self-discovery, from investing large profits to refunding and couponing.

One of the most interesting reasons to continue learning is the evidence suggesting that learning actually enhances mental well-being, physical health and in some cases longevity. Dr. Robert Samp, a physician and health educator at the University of Wisconsin Medical School, says "There is plenty of indication that taking courses is a beneficial activity contributing to good health."[12]

If this fact is true then there should be more and more healthy people around. According to Diane Stern, of the Adult Education Hotline in Westchester County, "People tend to be more goal oriented today than ever before. As a result not only is there a rising number of people getting involved in some sort of educational program, but there is a rising number of programs available."

This observation can be further illustrated in this parody I came across recently. You might have seen it. The sheet advertised some of the following continuing education courses:

SELF-IMPROVEMENT
Creative Suffering
Overcoming Peace of Mind
You and Your Birthmark
Whine Your Way to Alienation
Guilt Without Sex

BUSINESS AND CAREER
Money Can Make You Rich
"I Made $100 In Real Estate"
The Underachievers Guide to Very Small Business Opportunities

---

[12] Wilbur Cross, "Surprising Rx for a Richer Happier Life," *Reader's Digest*, Apr. 1982, p. 139.

HOME ECONOMICS
How You Can Convert Your Family Room Into A Garage
Cultivating Viruses In Your Refrigerator
1001 Uses for Your Vacuum Cleaner

HEALTH AND FITNESS
Creative Tooth Decay
Exorcism and Acne
Suicide and Your Health
Tap Dance Your Way to Social Ridicule

As an increasing number of people strive for self-education, an increasing number of educational institutions offer a larger listing of programs. Many universities, for instance, have satellite programs offered in communities, using local facilities. Some offer a battery of courses, others an entire degree and all are practically right in your own backyard. Parsons School of Design in NYC, for example, advertises degrees and non-accredited courses offered at suburban locations as much as forty minutes outside the city.

Also, many colleges and universities are now featuring courses in cooperation with public broadcasting stations. Degrees and credits in areas ranging from business management to oceanography can actually be obtained at home, over radio, TV and through newspapers. For more information on what's available in your vicinity write:

for TV courses:
International Consortium for Telecommunications in Learning
11767 Bonita Ave.
Owings Mills, MD 21117
(301) 356-5600

for radio:
National Public Radio
2025 M Street NW
Washington, DC 20036
(202) 822-2000

for radio & newspapers:
National Media Programs
University of California, San Diego
LaJolla, CA 92093
(619) 534-2230

Speaking of at-home study, if you're a self-motivated type that [ ]
to learn at your own pace, there are many correspondence schools
offer accredited training in subjects as varied as industrial arts and
gineering, jewelry design, retailing and computer programming. [ ]
urally courses of this sort vary in price, technique, content and s[ ]
So it's a good idea to thoroughly investigate those that interes[ ]

- Keep in mind, literature on each course is usually an advertisement written by a professional hard-hitter who knows exactly how to appeal to you.

- Don't be afraid to ask questions. Inquire about the course. Talk shop with other students, the teacher and the foundation sponsoring the program.

- If your expectations aren't being met, talk to the instructor to get more information or else ask him or her where you can get more specific details.

You can also use the following as a final check on whether the course, seminar, book or workshop will fulfill expectations:

- Does the school and course offering state specific objectives? If so, are they what you're looking for?

- Are the teaching methods compatible with your style of learning?

- Is the faculty/instructor an expert in the field(s)? And will you be able to interact easily with him or her?

- Is the school accredited?

- Is student progress and success recognized by employees and the educational community?
- Does the institution or program offer adequate facilities, equipment, hands-on training?
- Does the price seem reasonable for what you're getting?

Remember learning is a rewarding experience when the proper factors are present. If not, it can be draining, debilitating, and can cloud your feelings toward further education. It only takes a little extra effort to keep your opinion of education high. And that little extra effort can mean a world of difference.

UNCLE SAM WANTS YOU!

The media constantly bombard us with movies, TV shows, books, and articles depicting life in the military. Some leave us with the impression that it's a cold and rigid establishment. Others persuade us that it's, at times, a glamorous or even romantic endeavor. If you're considering the Army, Navy, Marines, etc. as one of your options to life after college, it's important to weigh each branch realistically, without any slants the media may impose.

Here are some of the advantages and disadvantages of the armed forces. We'll begin with a few major disadvantages. Take boot camp for instance. It's certainly no day at the beach. In order to learn discipline and responsibility, enlistees can expect tough drills, lectures, strenuous physical exercise. A tense instructor shouts loud commands that, at times, no matter how hard you try, you can't fulfill. Remember the movie *An Officer and a Gentleman?* Although there was a bit of Hollywood put in, many of the confrontations involving Richard Gere and Lou Gossett Jr. are typical.

For enlistees, military life has to come first. You may be required to spend long periods of time away from friends and family, on assignments that can be monotonous and often uncomfortable.

The armed services can be dangerous. Naturally during war there's the possibility of death, as well as the moral issue of killing. Even during peacetime, there are moments when your life and the lives of others are threatened. A fellow from my hometown was stationed in Germany after basic training. Fourteen months later he was killed. The cause? Some kind of accident during artillery training.

There is, of course, a brighter side to military life. For starters, joining the Army, Navy, Marines, etc. means serving your country in a useful way. Except in combat and combat-related jobs, it offers equal opportunities to women. The military will provide you with employment security and job advancement even in hard economic times. You'll achieve physical fitness, become more disciplined and learn important job skills. In fact, many college graduates sign up because the training and qualifications can later translate into the civilian work force.

You'll receive free dental and medical care, have good living conditions, food and adequate clothing (even if you aren't dressed in designer apparel). And you'll be entitled to a lot of little extras: like 30 days vacation annually, travel benefits, discount shopping in commissaries, free legal assistance and low-cost life insurance.

One of the most popular reasons for a person to enlist is the educational opportunities available. Since the military is extremely knowledge-oriented, they provide advance technical schooling, on-the-job training and even offer advanced degrees through military schools and in affiliation with accredited colleges and universities. To help you get the education you want, centers are set up on practically every installation, where trained counselors will coordinate a program for you! For college graduates this can mean obtaining an advanced degree free-of-charge while drawing full pay. Each year, for example, the Air Force selects 200 engineering officers to complete their masters and doctorate degrees in a variety of engineering disciplines. Your knowledge will be increased even further by opportunities to use the most sophisticated equipment available and most advanced technology around.

Or say you're interested in attending graduate school in the evenings. In return for your daytime commitment, most branches of the service pay a sizable percentage of your educational fees. (And if that's not enough, they'll even throw in an eight piece cutlery set, an amazing potato peeler and a 9×12 rug. Still not tempting? Well listen to this...)

As a college graduate you're eligible for officer training school. If you can meet the minimum physical and mental requirements, you can be quickly pushed up the ranks by completing a special training program for officers. And do you know what that means? More responsibility, greater respect, better benefits and higher pay. In fact, the Dept. of Labor claims that for people whose majors aren't in high demand, the military will pay as much as 50% more than a civilian employer. Not bad, eh? That's exactly what attracted Tom to military life. After he got his degree in marketing, he was having a difficult time making the career advances he wanted. The military offered him an officer training program, complete with all the extras. To Tom, the most appealing of all was the graduate education he'd receive in business. That's right — business.

It might surprise you to find out that the armed forces would actually provide training in a field like that. Most of us think the military is interested in technical personnel only. But in fact, there's hardly a job in the civilian world that's not found in the armed forces. Keep in mind, however, no matter how similar a job in the armed forces is to the civilian world, it still must incorporate a military lifestyle.

Ask yourself: Can I follow orders? Live out of a duffle bag? Kill another person? It's answers to such questions that will help you decide on a military commitment. It's true, the military can offer you a lot of invaluable advantages but they expect a lot in return. Can you forfeit certain freedoms? Are you willing to live away from friends and family? Can you make a three- to five-year commitment? On the following pages is a quick quiz that'll give you an idea if you're armed forces material. Why not take a few minutes to complete it? It may be all you'll need to alter some of your goals.

A MILITARY TEST[13]

Answer each of the questions below by checking the appropriate response. At the end of the quiz there is an explanation of how to grade yourself.

1. Can you cheerfully and willingly follow orders and instructions?
   - ☐ a) Yes, no problem.
   - ☐ b) Usually.
   - ☐ c) It depends.
   - ☐ d) No.

2. Can you accept criticism?
   - ☐ a) Sure.
   - ☐ b) Yes, but I don't like it.
   - ☐ c) Sometimes.
   - ☐ d) No way!

3. Can you be depended on to be on time for work and appointments?
   - ☐ a) Yes, always.
   - ☐ b) Almost always.
   - ☐ c) Sometimes.
   - ☐ d) Hardly at all.

4. Can you pay attention to details?
   - ☐ a) Yes.
   - ☐ b) Yes, but sometimes I slip.
   - ☐ c) If I'm interested.
   - ☐ d) No, who cares about picky details?

5. Can you discipline yourself to learn something new?
   - ☐ a) Yes, I love new challenges.
   - ☐ b) Yes, if necessary.
   - ☐ c) Well, okay, but I prefer the old.
   - ☐ d) No, why change?

[13] Texe W. Marrs, *You and the Armed Forces* (New York: Arco Publishing, Inc., 1983), pp. 6-8.

6. Can you adjust to being away from home?
 ☐ a) Yes, I love to travel.
 ☐ b) Yes, if I have to.
 ☐ c) Yes, if it's not too far from home or for too long.
 ☐ d) No, I'm a real "homebody."

7. Can you work well with others?
 ☐ a) Yes, no problem.
 ☐ b) Yes, but I prefer to work independently.
 ☐ c) Yes, if I like the others.
 ☐ d) No, I like to work alone.

8. Can you adjust to working long, erratic and unpredictable hours?
 ☐ a) Yes, I have a lot of energy.
 ☐ b) Yes, but I prefer a regular workweek.
 ☐ c) I can, but my boss must have a good reason for it.
 ☐ d) No, I'm a 9-5 person and I value my free time.

9. Are you physically fit?
 ☐ a) Yes, I'm in top shape.
 ☐ b) Yes, I'm in fairly good condition.
 ☐ c) I could be in better shape.
 ☐ d) No, not really and I detest anything "physical."

10. Can you tolerate someone else telling you how to dress and groom yourself?
 ☐ a) Yes, no problem.
 ☐ b) Yes, but I don't really like it.
 ☐ c) Only if it's absolutely necessary and it usually isn't in the military.
 ☐ d) No, I am an individual.

11. How much do you value your privacy?
 ☐ a) I am willing to totally sacrifice my privacy.
 ☐ b) A lot, but I understand that the military has a need to be deeply involved in most aspects of my life.
 ☐ c) I'm willing to let the military dictate to me "on the job," but they should stay out of my private life.
 ☐ d) Greatly and I don't like anyone "nosing" in my business or personal affairs.

12. Are you willing to participate in an armed conflict and, if necessary, to take the life of opposing enemy personnel?
 ☐ a) Yes.
 ☐ b) Yes, but reluctantly.
 ☐ c) Only if my life is threatened.
 ☐ d) No, I don't believe in war.

GRADING YOURSELF. For each (a) answer, give yourself a score of 4; each (b) gets 3 points; (c), two points; and a (d) response nets you 1 point. Total the number of points you earned from all 12 questions and evaluate yourself according to the following aptitude scale.

If you scored: Then your potential for success in military service is:

44 to 48 points Outstanding — military life for you will be a breeze.

39 to 43 points Excellent — the military and you will get along fine.

34 to 38 points Fair — both you and the service may become irritated and unhappy on occasion.

29 to 33 points Dubious — you may wish to consider not going into the service.

Are you still enthusiastic? Get all the facts first. Repeat — get all the facts first. Defense policies change quickly, so it's important to read everything you can get your hands on before enlisting. Check the library for current articles, military publications, and new books on the armed forces.

When you go speak to a recruiter, keep in mind they are required to fill an enlistment quota. Remember they are trained experts who believe in what they stand for and who, at times, make the Army, Navy, Coast Guard seem hard to pass up. In fact, in a recent news story on News 4, New York, reporter Steve Handelman disclosed that many recruiters mislead potential volunteers. For instance, before an enlistee signs up, he may be led to believe he'll definitely be trained for a specific job, when in reality, he can only be guaranteed a specific field, not occupation.

Consider the idea that recruitment pamphlets, speeches, films and interviews all put the armed services in the best possible light. After all, ever since 1973, when the government did away with the draft, the armed forces had to work harder to get volunteers.

Every time I sat down to write this chapter, I had a difficult time erasing my mind of the jingle "Be all that you can be, you can do it in the Army. . ." You think it's easy to get recruits? Not only do the armed services have to offer better career opportunities, higher education, rising financial support, but since it became voluntary, it spends over $160 million each year on advertising.

If you're tempted to enlist, it's not a bad idea to ask some veterans about their experiences and opinions. But keep in mind, people usually remember the very good or bad. Everything else usually gets forgotten. Whether the people you question were soured by Vietnam or gung-ho as a result of World War II, undoubtedly the features they liked or disliked may be for things that no longer exist.

It certainly makes sense to thoroughly research each branch of the military to find out what's best for you. And pay attention to details.

They are a good indication of what life will be like. Remember things like privacy will hardly exist, good grooming will be strictly enforced and homesickness is likely. Depending on the branch and field you're in, military personnel can work long, hard hours. At times there may be grueling physical requirements, at others a high demand for concentration and always a need for team spirit.

At this point, you may have stronger feelings about one branch of service over another, but do yourself a favor and consider all before you disregard any.

THE AIR FORCE

"Aim high!" This is the slogan for the youngest branch of the military, the Air Force. Established in 1947, it's responsible for the safety of soldiers on land and sea.

With the airplane as its major thrust, the Air Force guards against air attack. It provides space and aeronautic research and development, as well as a sophisticated network of radar detection.

Although many commercial pilots owe their training to the Air Force, there are more individuals in scientific, engineering, technical and non-technical jobs, than there are individuals who fly. In fact, the Air Force has a computerized system designed to match an enlistee's skills with related job openings. If an opportunity you want isn't available at the time you sign up, you're entitled to take advantage of their delay enlistment program. This allows you to enlist and wait up to 12 months for an opening that appeals to you.

Most Air Force recruits are not required to meet tough physical requirements. Rarely do commanders of the Air Force have to meet dress inspections or complete many of the usual drills other branches enforce. And living conditions are more like college dormitories than like typical barracks.

For more information, call the Air Force Recruiting Office nearest you (consult the phone book under U.S. Government — Air Force). Or write:

> Hq. U.S. Air Force Recruiting Service
> Randolph Air Force Base
> TX 78150

THE ARMY

Now *you* can battle with the jingle, "Be all that you can be . . ." if in fact, it's the Army you're interested in. I'm still having trouble getting the song out of my mind. Maybe I'll replace it with "Look for the union label . . ."

The Army is the largest and oldest of all five branches of service. Founded by Continental Congress in 1775, the Army is stationed worldwide in places like Alaska, Hawaii, Panama, Germany, Korea and, of course, the continental U.S. Since one-third of the entire force is stationed overseas, the Army offers many opportunities to travel.

Like the Air Force, this branch also has a computerized program where your qualifications and interests are matched with available openings. Also it has a delayed entry policy whereby you can wait for the most suitable position.

The Army differs from the Air Force, for instance, by putting a much heavier emphasis on physical training. Yet it offers comfortable housing, advanced facilities, competitive benefits and pay.

For details call an Army recruiter listed in the phone book under U.S. Government — Army. Or write:

> Headquarters U.S. Army Recruiting Commander
> Fort Sheridan, IL 60037

THE MARINES

They didn't get the motto "first to fight" for nothing. If it's the Marine Corps you're leaning towards, get ready for the toughest training of all military branches.

Under the direction of the U.S. Navy, the Marine Corps has been in existence since 1775. And since that time, it has carried over a traditional military regime of the most rigid, demanding physical training, self-disciplined, sacrificing mental training.

Because the Marine Corps takes on amphibious responsibilities your assignment usually begins aboard a Navy vessel and may develop either on land or sea in one of the occupational fields the Marines offer: from motor transport to avionics, combat arms to electronics. This branch is divided into two principal sections: the Operating Forces and Supporting Establishment.

To see if the Marine Corps best suits you, contact the U.S. Government — Marine Corps found in your telephone directory. Or write:

> Marine Corps Opportunities
> PO Box 38901
> Los Angeles, CA 90038

THE NAVY

For the right person, the Navy can be "more than a job, an adventure." As a protection defensively and offensively for the seas, the Navy offers a large number of careers for people in almost every occupation. Whether you work in medical supply or food service, as a telephone operator or pilot, this branch can take you all over the world and expose you to new places, people and technology. Whether you'll choose life ashore, on submarines, ships or flattops, the Navy offers over 60 occupational fields and schooling opportunities from which to choose.

Again, for more information look in your phone book under U.S. Government — Navy or call:

> Commander, Navy Recruiting Command
> 3837 Pennsylvania Ave., SE
> Washington, DC 20020
> 1-800-327-NAVY (327-6289)

THE COAST GUARD

It might surprise you to find out that the Coast Guard is actually a branch of the military. Although it falls under the jurisdiction of the Department of Transportation, in wartime it protects the U.S. coastline under the Navy's supervision.

The Coast Guard is the smallest branch of the armed forces. Composed of approximately 38,000 members, it maintains navigation and rescue missions, collects oceanographic data for environmental research, enforces pollution regulation, offers boat safety programs and a lot more.

Their slogan "semper paratus" which means "always ready" suits them perfectly since each year they receive about 70,000 calls for assistance in water-related incidents. It's been estimated that they save about 4,200 persons from death annually, aid another 140,000, and save about $280 million of endangered property.

A special feature of the Coast Guard is that you can go through boot camp with a friend of the same sex.

On assignment you can expect to be stationed mainly in large cities with heavily populated coast lines. At these sites you'll perform many of the same duties the Navy handles; however, benefits are not as good in this branch of service.

For more information call the Coast Guard. The number can be found in your telephone directory listed under the Department of Transportation.

SOME FACTS ON ENLISTMENT

Do you meet the minimum requirements for enlistment? If you're fresh out of college most likely you do. Enlistees must be:

- over 17 years old, maximum age range is 28–35
- a U.S. citizen
- in good physical condition
- of good moral standing
- without a criminal record
- a high school graduate — no problem here! In fact, you're eligible for officer training since you're a college graduate.

Did you realize you must take an entrance exam before enlisting?

It's called the Armed Services Vocational Aptitude Battery. It's a 2½ hour aptitude test that measures knowledge like word power, reasoning, mechanical comprehension, etc. The ASVAB is not an intelligence exam, rather it helps determine the career fields and job specialities you're capable of handling. Books are available on the test. One you might want to look into is *Practice for Army Placement Tests* published by Arco Publishing Co., 1982.

Did you know there are a number of enlistment options to consider before signing up? Before making a commitment check into unit of choice, station of choice, advanced rank, etc. Of course, your choices may not always be available. After you enlist, if the area and job you've chosen isn't open, something else will be suggested by a counselor. You're under no obligation to take the new option. So think things over before you sign anything. Perhaps another branch of service will have an opening for you!

RELATED CIVILIAN CAREERS

Don't be disappointed if you're suddenly realizing the military isn't for you. Maybe you can't pass the physical exam or perhaps you can't really make a three year commitment. You still have one last option related to the Armed Services, the Dept. of Defense employs about 1,000,000 men and women to work for the military in a civilian capacity.

For more information write the Public Information Office of the Department of Defense in these branches:

Department of Defense
Chief Staffing & Support Programs
Director for Personnel & Security
Room 3B347
The Pentagon
Washington, DC 20301

Air Force
Public Information Office
1947th Administrative Support Group
Department of Air Force
The Pentagon
Washington, DC 20330

Army
Department of the Army Civilian Personnel Center
200 Stovall St.
Hoffman II
Attn: Career Management Operations Directorate
Special Actions Division
Alexandria, VA 22332

Marine Corps
Commandant of the Marine Corps (MPS-30)
Headquarters
U.S. Marine Corps
Washington, DC 20380

Navy
Naval Civilian Personnel Command
800 North Quincy St.
Arlington, VA 22203

Coast Guard
contact through Federal Job Information Centers

TRAVEL A NEW HIGHWAY.

I was in Greece not too long ago, roaming through some village shops, when I came upon one that was especially intriguing. It sold jewelry, which always attracts me, and it had traditional Greek music blaring in the background. I strolled in, smiled at the shopkeeper and then snapped my fingers above my head in rhythm with the song. The shopkeeper grabbed my hand and we danced down the aisle laughing, singing and just plain having a good time. I spoke no Greek, he spoke no English, but when the song ended we kissed each other and I went on my way. It was an experience I'll always cherish. There I was, clear across the globe, in a country where their alphabet isn't even the same. Yet I exchanged a joyous, spontaneous moment with a stranger.

Meeting people of different backgrounds is just one of the many rewards of traveling. If you're considering a trip, now that you've graduated from college, most likely you know its other benefits. Traveling is a terrific way to delve into the field you've just studied. Certainly for those of you who graduated as archeology majors, traveling can be a way to turn text book knowledge into first-hand experience. Going on a dig or studying ancient ruins can help you gain valuable career-oriented knowledge. For art students who yearn to see Van Gogh at his best, why not save for a trip to the Van Gogh museum in Amsterdam?

Traveling builds character. Learning different cultures and customs can expand a person's outlook on life and people. It's one way to explore a new place to live. If you were dissatisfied spending the last four years as a city dweller, traveling is a great way to investigate other areas. It can broaden interests. For avid bird-watchers to water-logged scuba divers, what better way to catch a glimpse of a rare species?

Now that you've graduated from college there's practically no time as ideal to take advantage of the pleasures of travel — you're not committed to school anymore and your responsibilities are probably as minimal as they'll ever be. Yet even though the timing may seem perfect, traveling at this point in your life can pose some threats. For starters, you may face some opposition. There was no one more disappointed than my father to hear I was going to Europe after I graduated.

He'd spent quite a bit on my education, "What about a career?"

Depending on the length of time you plan to spend, traveling can gobble some of the important years you could be devoting to other goals. I have to admit, although being in Europe was a terrific experience for me, when I returned I felt a little disheartened calling friends who were already involved in a career and well into grad school.

Traveling at times can be life-threatening. With all the hijackings and air crashes we hear about, it's only natural to be concerned for our own safety. However, we must keep fears like these in perspective.

So even though traveling has numerous rewards, there are some disadvantages too. If you've weighed all the pros and cons, and still have wanderlust, here are a number of factors to consider before heading north, south, east or west.

DESTINATION

Wouldn't it be nice to say "I'm going to California in September, England in November, scooting to Switzerland in January then on to Japan next spring?" Unfortunately very few graduates have the luxury of traveling where they want, when they want. That's why it's so important to choose a location that will fulfill you in three ways.

1) The destination you choose should satisfy a specific need. Maybe you're looking for the kind of relaxation two weeks in the sun will provide? Perhaps you'd like an adventure skiing the Rockies? Or better yet, a self-enlightening experience in an Indian ashram? Whatever your reason for travel, it's imperative to select a locale that has the natural resources, climate, social conditions, educational facilities, commerce, etc. to give you what you're looking for.

Two friends of mine took advantage of reduced rates and flew to Ft. Lauderdale off-season. The trip would have been fine except it lacked all the excitement of beach parties, discos, tourists from other schools and colleges. They spent two glorious weeks amongst natives three times their age.

2) Choosing a destination should be dependent upon the amount of time you can stay. If you've ever seen the movie *If It's Tuesday This Must Be Belgium*, you'll know how important it is to coordinate your itinerary with the amount of time you'll be staying. Racing from site to site trying to cram in everything within an unreasonable time frame can be disastrous. If you only have seven days to tour all of Europe, why not reconsider and spend the week in Amsterdam, for example?

3) Finally your financial status should always be considered when selecting a destination. What good is going to the Bahamas this Easter if you can't afford the extras? Maybe Ft. Lauderdale will give you what you're looking for. Or what purpose would a study trip to China serve if you can't swing their cost of living?

TRANSPORTATION

So how are you going to reach your destination? Depending on the amount of time and money you have, getting to your destination can be part of the fun. Herb loves to bike ride. Practically every weekend he rides further and further away. In fact, when he graduated from college, a friend bet him $250 that he couldn't make it from New York to California in a week's time. Although he gave it all he had, Herb lost the bet. It took him ten days to get to San Francisco. The $250 may break Herb now, but he's left with experiences money could never buy.

Let's not forget cruises. I've heard some great stories of people taking the cruise of a lifetime. Some cruises accommodate a special interest like wine-tasting, music and art, while others are just a great way to relax, eat and eat some more. If you're considering a cruise make sure you do ample research before making reservations. Study the trip's itinerary, consider days on board vs. days at port and ask about living accommodations, activities, service and most importantly, the age of the other passengers. Better do some research.

Certainly one of the most popular ways to travel is by plane. If that's the mode of transportation you opt for, you can make reservations by calling a travel agent or the airlines directly. When you do, keep in mind that airfares are usually reduced during weekdays (Monday–Thursday) and at night, after 9 P.M. Some airlines offer cheaper rates to a destination off-season, like my buddies who went to Ft. Lauderdale. And there's something called excursion fares designed for travelers overseas. If you stay a certain length of time you'll save on airfare. Usually the longer you stay the cheaper your rates. And for travel within the U.S., don't forget to ask about supersaver airfares. If you purchase flight tickets seven days before departure and stay at least seven days, you can save as much as 30–50% over regular prices.

Of course, getting to and from a destination isn't the only transportation you have to consider. After all, if you fly, how will you get to the hotel from the airport and vice versa? If you hike, how will you get to your starting point and back again? You've got to research what's available ahead of time to plan accordingly. Thankfully I had an experienced travel agent when I visited London. Her suggestion to buy a bus ticket in advance saved my friends and me a lot of aggravation.

Transportation is certainly a matter of taste, time and money and a major consideration when planning to travel.

LIVING ACCOMMODATIONS

Did you have the kind of parents who constantly asked "Where are you going and who are you staying with?" If so, you'll probably feel more comfortable making living arrangements before you head out the door. If you didn't hear questions like that, it's still not a bad idea to consider accommodations in advance. Not only will it make you feel more secure but you'll avoid roaming unfamiliar streets at unsavory hours, looking for somewhere to sleep.

Reserving a room in advance is wise if you're going somewhere during peak season, such as a festival or convention of some sort. My husband and I packed the car and headed for Newport, Rhode Island, one weekend. It seemed like a pleasant thing to do. But we went up without any hotel arrangements. When we reached Newport we looked for a place to stay, without luck. Since we had a tent and sleeping bags as backup, we decided to eat, drink and worry about sleeping later. There we were at 2 A.M. touring Jamestown, Newport and everywhere in the vicinity looking for shelter. Finally I asked a policeman; he suggested we just pitch the tent. The next morning we woke up to thousands of people arranging lawn chairs. It turned out we had the best spot possible to watch the Newport Tall Ships Festival. That wasn't good enough for me, though; I still wanted a shower.

Most large cities feature accommodations of all qualities and price ranges. At this stage of your life, you'll probably opt for the most inexpensive hotels — that is, unless you can stay with friends or family. If your trip will be rather low budget, be smart and check out a place before you give an okay. Get brochures, call the tourist bureau, Chamber of Commerce and ask friends or professionals who have been there recently. Since the quality of hotels and motels changes quickly, don't rely on stale opinions.

On the other hand, if you are the adventurous type who doesn't mind the hassle of hunting for a room once you arrive, do make certain to do some research ahead of time. Again, call the Chamber of Commerce in advance, the tourist bureau, ask friends and professionals for advice and read some books before you go. Then when you do find a place that seems reasonable, take the added precaution to check it out first. During that trip to Greece mentioned at the beginning of this chapter, we were pressed for a room. We went to a local hotel that seemed to our liking; the lobby was clean, the place looked decent. But after we paid the hotel clerk, he brought us two blocks away to a dingy room where we had to share a bathroom with six other people. So much for live and learn.

MEALS

Whether eating is something you look forward to or not, it's something you have to plan for while traveling. Planning doesn't mean you have to make reservations for every meal before you leave home. It means that the price of eating during your stay must be figured into your travel expenses.

People who aren't very experimental, or who are on a very strict diet, often choose to take advantage of meals their hotel offers. In fact, if you're going to a place where water and food standards aren't as high as ours, it's not a bad idea to take advantage of the hotel meal plan. The bigger hotels usually follow better health codes. But keep in mind, when you're on a fixed plan you're also on a fixed schedule to be back at the hotel at specific times. Otherwise you're obligated to pay for a meal you didn't devour.

For those of you who are adventurous eaters, traveling can be an eye-opening experience. It's one way to learn more about local customs and tradition and try new spices, blends and combinations. Do yourself one favor first. Before you go anywhere find out about health standards.

In addition, it's smart to find out the approximate price range of dining out. Naturally most locations have restaurants that run the gamut from the very expensive to the very affordable. But if you're on a strict budget it'll be to your advantage to find out a general cost of living. In a fit of desperation once, I actually spent $7 for a small jar of peanut butter.

Even if your eating arrangements are set, make a habit of carrying something to eat and drink while traveling. Unexpected delays like traffic jams, circling airports, off-schedule trains, look much better with something good to munch on. Before I boarded a three-hour train ride to Mestre, Italy, I had the most delicious Italian ham on a loaf of crunchy bread. Every bite was wonderful. The train came, I got on and had the most terrific thirst I've ever had in my life. The train was hot, the car was packed and the Italian ham salty. Across the aisle from me was a little girl slurping a cold, dripping soda and I actually thought of kidnapping her to have a sip.

ITINERARY

Planning an itinerary is a good way to get the most from your trip. You wouldn't take a college course without first discovering what it offers, what you'll learn or what's required of you. So why not give your trip the same consideration? Some people plot a rigid schedule of day-to-day things to do, sites to see and places to eat, while others determine a general course of action, then leave the rest to fate.

Whichever you opt for, planning an itinerary can be fun but does require a fair amount of research before you go. Find out what's available in the country, city, town you're visiting. Check what the outlying areas offer. Then make a list of things you'd like to accomplish. Whether you're a rigid planner or a flexible one, get an idea of how long it will take to travel from one place to another. Decide approximately how long you'd like to stay at each place, then work out a reasonable agenda of when, why and how you'll be seeing Big Sur, touring Beverly Hills and visiting Aunt Mary.

As mentioned before, you can get the necessary information you need by asking your travel agent, reading brochures, books and articles, calling the Chamber of Commerce and tourist offices. These sources will tell you what's in season, when sites are open, what tours are offered. They may also provide important extras, like the time frame in which a country or city operates.

All in all, an important step to planning a successful trip is planning a successful itinerary. The extra time you take to do some careful research will not only insure you'll see the Louvre, the Taj Mahal, get to the Statue of Liberty — it's a great way to learn vital particulars about the place you're visiting.

DETAILS

The research you do before you travel can make or break your trip. Let's use your blow dryer for example. In certain countries electrical wattage and outlets are different from ours. That means you'd need an adapter and converter to use your blow dryer effectively. Imagine getting ready for your big day in Venice, only to discover you can't style your hair? (That's okay, your hairdo would match the rest of you since you wouldn't be able to use your iron or your electric shaver either.)

Consider tipping standards. In some countries a waiter's tip is included in the restaurant bill. In others, you have to leave a certain percentage, while some don't require a tip at all.

In some places clothing sizes are based on a different scale than ours and exportation laws have varying restrictions. Even social customs may differ. Take, for instance, Johannesburg. If your car has a flat tire it's customary to remain in the car until help arrives.

Doing research before you leave can acquaint you with a location's cultural differences, religious and social customs, economic, educational and business protocol. Of course, if you're traveling within the U.S. your research won't have to be as extensive as if you're going overseas — but it certainly will help you to reach your travel goals.

The amount of research you'll have to do also depends on whether you're going alone, with a friend or on a guided tour. If you're traveling alone, you'll have the burden of doing some heavy-duty work before you leave. Then when you arrive there's the added responsibility of changing currency, coordinating arrival and departure times, confirming living accommodations, etc. These duties can be divided among traveling companions, if you're traveling with others. Or better yet, if you'll be traveling with a group, usually the tour escort will explain the necessary arrangements beforehand and help you with particulars when you reach your destination.

So the research you have to do to make your trip successful relies on two factors. For starters, it depends on where you're going and how familiar you are with your destination. Secondly, it depends on what kind of trip you're taking: a trip alone, with friends, or with a professional travel club or tour group.

ARRANGEMENTS

If you prefer to take matters into your own hands — by calling airlines, hotels, sight-seeing tours directly — be ready to spend a lot of time selecting, reserving, scheduling and rescheduling. Prices and the quality of flights, cruises, living accommodations change rather quickly in this industry. To make matters more confusing, don't expect to find all the information you need in one source. There are hundreds of books written on the subject all offering different perspectives. So arranging your own trip may sound great now, but it may be an undertaking that's far too tedious to handle. After all, people spend years working to become proficient travel agents, and even with the facts at their fingertips, many still have trouble.

If you would rather have a professional handle your excursion there are several options to choose from. First, why not consider a good travel agent? The word *good* is stressed here because many can foul up details just as easily as a nonprofessional. Since the travel industry hasn't established formalized standards for their agents, it can be difficult to determine whether or not a person will be terrific.

If you're a little uneasy about selecting one, why not ask for recommendations from friends and relatives? Or why not call the Better Business Bureau in your area? They'll tell you if any complaints have been filed against an agency. And keep an eye open for the initials ASTA on the agency's window. They stand for American Society of Travel Agents, an organization that requires its members to be in operation a minimum of three years and to have written at least $500,000 worth of business in the year preceding their initiation. In addition, see if the agent you're dealing with has the initials CTC after his name. This indicates he has successfully completed an 18-month to 2-year course given by the Institute of Certified Travel Agents.

Another way to decide if you've chosen a savvy agent is if he has taken a trip recently to the place you're considering. His firsthand experience will be terrific background to help you choose living accommodations, tours, transportation, a daily itinerary and connecting flights. A good travel agent should also provide information on getting a passport, visa and immunization shots.

Usually larger agencies are exposed to more of what's available so they're often better equipped to advise you. For specialized needs, such as exotic vacations and travel for the handicapped, your best bet is to go to an agency that specializes in such trips.

You can aid a travel agent in doing a professional job. By providing him with important facts — the kind of trip you want to take, the budget you can afford, the time of year you want to go and the interests you want to explore — you and he can plan an ideal jaunt.

One more fact to consider: travel agents are usually paid by commissions from airlines, car rental firms, tour operators and the like.

Make sure you select one you don't have to pay.

Travel clubs are another option to planning your own trip. Usually women's clubs, men's clubs, sporting and hobby groups, school alumni organizations, and recreation associations offer excursions with reduced rates. At a discount of 5% – 20%, you can take a great trip with people who share similar interests. Or why not start a club of your own? By getting a small group together (10–15 people) you'll not only get discounts from hotels and sight-seeing establishments but you may even be entitled to some free transportation tickets.

Group tours are also available from wholesale tour operators. Like travel clubs, these tours offer quantity discounts and are arranged to accommodate almost everyone's tastes. Tour groups are designed by professionals, who are aware of the best deals around and know the ins and outs of travel and the travel industry. So making reservations with a reputable tour operator will save you a lot of time, money and research work. But before you commit yourself be certain that you are fully aware of what the tour operator offers, what's included in the trip, as well as what's not included!

HEALTH PRECAUTIONS

I've often thought a good selling point to write on my résumé is that I only get sick on weekends and vacations. Unfortunately this is usually the case with me and probably one of the reasons why I make an effort to stay employed. Even if you only rarely get ill, it can happen while traveling. Believe me, there's nothing worse than getting sick away from home. That's why it's so important to take precautions that will increase your chances of having a safe and healthy trip.

If you're planning to be away for an extended period of time, get an overall checkup by your doctor and dentist. Each year buddies of mine take a fishing trip to Manitoba. They board a small sea plane in Montreal and are dropped off at a cabin somewhere in the wilderness. There are no phones, food or people. The only way they can contact the real world is by lighting a flair and waiting for a plane to fly overhead. Last year one of my friends developed an agonizing toothache he had to suffer with for two days before he was picked up and taken to a professional. Had he been to a dentist before his trip, this entire episode could have been avoided. So visit your dentist and have any necessary dental work completed before you go. Then make an appointment to see your doctor. If you're presently taking medication, bring an ample supply with you and ask the doctor for the prescription's generic name. If you lose your medicine it can be replaced with less trouble.

Tell the doctor where you're going and ask if it's necessary to be immunized. If so, be sure to get shots at least one month prior to your departure. Not only do some innoculations require two injections, sometimes two weeks apart, but you might also be one of the unfortunate people who have a bad reaction.

If your doctor isn't sure whether shots should be administered, call your local health department or write the Public Health Service, U.S. Department of Health, Education & Welfare, Atlanta, GA 30333 or call (404) 329-3311. Health information for international travelers will be provided.

It's also a good idea to have your doctor fill out a wallet-sized medical card for you. This lists your medical history (allergies, medications, blood type, etc.) on a strip of microfilm. For more information and an application form, send a self-addressed stamped envelope to the National Safety Council, Health and Safety Awareness Center, Order Dept., 444 North Michigan Ave., Chicago, IL 60611, (312) 527-4800.

In addition, ask your doctor to recommend a health care professional in the city where you'll be staying. Or write or phone the International Association for Medical Assistance to Travellers, 736 Center St., Lewiston, NY 14902 (716) 754-4883. They'll send a worldwide list of reputable English-speaking doctors. If you become ill and need medical attention, a hotel concierge can usually recommend someone and so can a tour escort, a local pharmacy or a U.S. embassy or consulate.

That takes care of major catastrophes. But what about minor discomforts? I woke one morning in Venice with fingers the size of baseball mitts. This is a slight exaggeration, but certainly an uncomfortable condition that I probably could have avoided had I been more selective about the foods I ate.

A person doesn't have to be a world traveler to know that in some places sanitary codes are not as rigid as they should be. Throughout your trip, be cautious of the sanitary conditions in the places you eat and drink. Since water can carry parasites, bacteria and virus, stay away from water, ice cubes, fresh fruits and vegetables. This is not to say you can't bite into a cold, refreshing kumquat or drink a thirst-quenching iced tea, just be sure when you do it's in a place where water and food standards are high. Since cooking destroys most food problems, eat meat and fish that are well-cooked. Be aware that heavily spiced foods often mask contamination. And watch things like mayonnaise, cream fillings and fresh milk.

No matter where you go, carry along a first aid kit. Include remedies for constipation, diarrhea, motion sickness and nausea. Remember to pack aspirin, antiseptics, Band-Aids, tweezers, a thermometer, insect repellent, cough medicine, vitamins and anything else you need to stay well. These should be carried with you and not tucked in a suitcase that can get lost or stolen.

PACKING

Let a world traveler who doubles as a fashion plate tell you what to take on your next trip. We'll just concentrate on the basics.

There are a lot of variables to consider when packing for travel. Most are common sense. First of all, the purpose of your trip dictates certain things to include. If you're going on a ski weekend naturally you'll bring ski equipment and warm clothing. For a business trip, you'll definitely need business clothes. Claire flew from New York City to Seattle recently on business. Upon arrival she realized the bag she packed her shoes in was left at home. Since all stores were closed, she considered limping into her meeting with sneakers on and explaining to clients that she was recovering from foot surgery. Instead she borrowed shoes from the hotel manager. (Good thing the manager was a woman.)

Packing also depends on the duration of your trip. Usually the longer you're away, the more you'll want and need. If you're packing for a lengthy stay, find out how much luggage you're allowed. Standards vary among airlines, cruise ships, trains and buses.

The place you're traveling to has something to do with what you'll bring. So do the events you'll attend. In some countries specific dress codes are strictly enforced. In the Vatican, for example, women are not allowed into the Sistine Chapel without covering their heads, shoulders and arms.

Let's not forget climate. It may be warmer where you're headed so pack accordingly.

Whether a dapper set of luggage best suits you or a rugged backpack, belongings can get lost or stolen en route. If this happens immediately report the loss to transportation officials.

One final point: as an extra precaution, don't pack first aid, prescriptions, eyeglasses, documents and money in your luggage. Use a separate carry-on bag. If luggage does get lost or stolen at least you'll have the real necessities.

PROTECTION

We spent an entire day selecting and buying souvenirs. We walked in and out of every shop in the village and haggled with practically every vendor around. At the end of the day we dropped our treasures at the hotel and the next morning we noticed everything we bought, and I mean everything, was gone.

Let's face it. No matter where you go on earth, there's a fair share of people who are dishonest. Whether we were robbed by natives or other tourists really doesn't matter. The fact is we were ripped off. So please take some precautions.

As far as money goes, experts will tell you (and I don't mean Karl Malden only) that the safest way to carry funds is by using traveler's checks. If they're lost or stolen they can be replaced and, since there's no expiration date, they're always valid. Some stores even offer a 4–20% discount if payment is made this way.

Since many credit cards are internationally accepted now, you might consider using them as a backup system. In fact, several provide a limited check cashing service for cardholders. But be careful. These too can be stolen.

Being robbed is only one of many crimes a person can fall victim to. That's why it's so important to leave a detailed itinerary back home, of where you'll be and when. If anything happens back at the homestead friends and relatives can get in touch. And if anything should happen to you during your stay, there'll be a way to track your course. It's also a good idea to have someone you trust know your passport identification number and the numbers of your traveler's checks. If they're lost or stolen, at least you'll be able to call home for particulars you'll need.

But crime works both ways. You don't have to be a hardened criminal to break the law. In some countries the laws are easier to break than you'd imagine: "...according to John Caufield, a former spokesman for the State Department's Bureau of Consular Affairs, about 3,000 Americans are arrested in foreign countries annually on a variety of charges, and just under half that number will actually be imprisoned."[14]

Don't let this statistic frighten you. Let it convince you to be cautious. Whether you're traveling within the U.S. or traveling on foreign soil, you have to abide by local rules. Although you may be familiar with the laws here, don't assume they'll be the same where you're headed. In some places just taking snapshots in a restricted area can be a felony. And, unlike legal procedures in the U.S., you may be considered guilty until proven innocent.

So why not do yourself a favor? Read some books and articles on the laws of the country you're visiting. Memorize your passport ID number and where it was issued and have a listing of your traveler's check numbers. Be very cautious and if something terrible should happen overseas remember to call the American embassy or consulate nearest you. They'll contact English-speaking lawyers, make provisions for you to call home and do their best to get you out of your predicament.

REQUIREMENTS

Are you traveling overseas? You'll need a number of documents to get out of the country and back again, and to work and drive during your visit. A passport allows a U.S. citizen to leave and re-enter the country. You can obtain one by applying to the Passport Agency of the U.S. State

---

[14] David C. Ruffin, "Protecting Yourself on Foreign Soil," *Black Enterprise*, Mar. 1984, p. 72.

Department, the clerk of the Federal Court and even at some local post offices. Be certain to allow ample time, at least four weeks, to get one.

There's a big demand for black market passports so guard yours carefully. As mentioned before memorize your passport ID number and the place where it was issued. If it is lost or stolen you can call the U.S. embassy or consulate nearest you and provide the necessary data. For details on passports write for a copy of "You and Your Passport," Passport Agency, U.S. Department of State, Washington, D.C. 20524, or call (202) 783-8200.

Depending on the diplomatic relations and agreements we have with other countries, you may also need a visa to travel to and from a specific country. About 100 nations require U.S. citizens to have them. Getting a visa can take anywhere from one day to four weeks, so allow ample time. For more information ask your travel agent or call the U.S. Department of State. They'll be able to advise you on obtaining a working visa for employment overseas.

About 100 countries also require visitors to have an international driver's license, to operate a motor vehicle in their territory. If you're planning to drive, call the local office of your state automobile club. They'll provide all the necessary details.

It's better to apply for your international driver's permit in person. Applying through the mail takes a lot more time plus it means that you have to mail your U.S. driver's license.

AT THE HOMESTEAD

Don't get so caught up in the excitement of traveling that you forget responsibilities at home. For those of you who have a pet, get someone you can rely on to feed and care for it. I have a dog who's considered a member of the family. He goes to work with my husband every day and even travels with us when possible. So you can imagine how frustrated I was, 1,000 miles from home, knowing that the person who was taking care of my pooch locked him in the house all weekend to go to Montauk. Don't make the same mistake. Get someone reliable.

If you have your own apartment have the post office hold your mail or have someone take it in each day along with the newspaper. Put your lights on timers, lock all doors and windows, turn off gas jets and electrical appliances and don't forget to cover any important bills you may have. Bon voyage!

A FINAL WORD: Appendix B lists a number of sources for free information, inside tips and helpful hints.

TALKING SHOP:
JOB vs. CAREER.

Now for the chapter you've all been waiting for — or most of you anyway. It's on finding a job. If it's a biggie for you, all I can say is, it
was equally so for me. There are countless professionals available willing to give advice. And there is unlimited information to forge through
to be well informed on the subject. I've been through most of it. And
frankly, I can't figure out how a lot of working people I know, who
haven't followed many of these rules, ever got their jobs in the first
place. This just proves that although job-hunting techniques are endless, if you disregard many, you can still find a good one. But there's no
guarantee it will be easily found or will be the best for you. The odds
are in your favor if you stick to the proven methods and strategies out-
lined in this chapter. So here are some tips, ideas, examples and plenty
of them to help you become a productive, fulfilled member of the work
force.

At this point in life you probably have an idea of how you'll approach the working world. But are you realistic? Many recent college
graduates have misconceptions of how industry views a recent graduate. As a result they find themselves in some pretty sticky situations.
Among the most common delusions are the following:

"I have the world on a string." Getting your diploma may give you
a great feeling of satisfaction — and rightly so. You accomplished a big
goal. But don't let that feeling trick you into thinking you can get whatever you want, whenever you want it. While you should be proud of
the degree you earned, it is by no means a ticket to the best the world
has available. Nor is it any indication that you have a special talent to
offer humanity. So feel proud that you're a graduate, but keep in mind
it's only the beginning.

"I know more and am better than others." Of course this isn't the
kind of statement people usually make, but many graduates give this
impression. Some tend to be cocky now that they have a sheepskin and
a little knowledge to back them. But in the business world people don't
respect a "know-it-all" unless he does, in fact, know a lot. For those of
you who are just entering the work force there are important lessons,

techniques and practices yet to be discovered. Your diploma is one of many ways to help you start the search.

"*I know absolutely nothing.*" This, too, isn't a statement you would normally make, but like the preceding example it's an impression you may leave. Thinking you are inept is as big a mistake as acting cocky and overconfident. Although you may not have all the skills necessary for a particular position, you still have time to learn them. When you begin a job, no matter how menial, employers know that you'll need time to pick up the ins and outs.

"*I have to work in the field I studied.*" Says who? Just because you majored in accounting doesn't mean you're trapped within that discipline. Your college education has given you a broad background in many other areas as well. If you find something else that interests you more, go for it. And take your accounting knowledge with you. There will be plenty of ways you can translate those skills into your new field. Look at Dave. He graduated with a degree in marketing. His first job was writing for a local newspaper. He felt a little sorry that he wasn't applying his marketing knowledge. But he made up for it. Three years later Dave began writing a house organ for a company in Seattle. And guess what? Because it was a management consulting firm, the job demanded each candidate have a business degree, as well as writing experience. Dave fit right in.

"*Now that I'm looking for work I have to pursue a career.*" Is that what your mother told you? No way do you have to feel compelled to become Mr. or Ms. Corporate America — at least not now. In fact, getting a job that pays the rent and gives you the time to pursue other goals can be just as rewarding, or even more so, as a job that looks like it'll thrust you up the corporate ladder. In other words, there are two ways to approach business: you can pursue a field you think will become your life's work, your career; or you can take a job that will provide you with the support you need to pursue other goals.

In a recent speech, Rebecca Jann makes the distinction quite well. "The way you can tell that you have a career is if you can hardly wait to get to work. If you dread going to work most days, then you don't have a career, you have a job. And you might as well look for another job which is easier or which pays better. For many very happy and successful people, jobs are just ways to finance their true callings. Their real careers are what they do in their spare time."[15]

So if you're looking for work of any kind the following information will help. It's divided into two chapters. Chapter 7 focuses on careers; Chapter 8 on the temporary job or non-career-related job.

[15] Rebecca C. Jann, "What They Should Have Told Me When I Was a Senior," *Vital Speeches of the Day*, 1 Nov. 1983, p. 52.

THE CAREER-TYPE JOB

Finding a career-type job is serious business. Millions of dollars are spent on research, books, seminars and services that instruct us how to get a fulfilling job and how to climb the corporate ladder. Although most propose to give you the secret formula to the best position, highest pay, fastest ascent — the truth is there are no big mysteries as to how to land the job you want. It takes plenty of persistence, perseverance and a lot of hard work that, at times, can make job-hunting a career in and of itself.

Of course, there are methods for seeking work that are usually more effective than others. This chapter will present a variety of ways you can find employment. And many statistics confirm that the outcome of your job hunt will probably be positive. *The New York Times* recently carried a story that included the following quote: "The job picture for (college) seniors is brighter and employment outlook promising. . . for technical and professional employees and generally positive for other groups, says the Bureau of National Affairs (a private firm based in Washington, D.C., that publishes many specialized reports in the areas of business, economics, politics and law).[16]

So let's get to work!

Choosing a Position

As if the decision to pursue a career weren't tough enough, now you have to determine which career is right for you. Although finding the ideal job can be a lifetime process and can mean shifting from industry to industry, position to position, company to company — the fact is, you have to start somewhere.

For some of you choosing a field, position or company to work for is no trouble. But for the majority who are totally confused or even a tinge uncertain, the decision can be grueling. Not only do your own thoughts keep you spinning, but you're constantly being bombarded by advice from friends, relatives and the media — which only makes matters worse. Like this excerpt from *U.S. News & World Report*, ". . . employers say that the number one problem with people coming in for their first job is that they don't know what kind of position they're looking for."[17]

So where do you begin? The search starts once again with self-assessment. If you're in tune with your goals and values, if you've identified your interests, skills and abilities, then the right move is to focus on a field, company and position that utilizes your qualifications. This is nothing you haven't heard before, but it could be something

---

[16] Shirley Fader Sloan, "Finding Hidden Jobs," *Working Woman*, June 1984, p. 42.

[17] "That First Job: Finding It and Getting Ahead," *U.S. News & World Report*, 6 July 1981, p. 67.

you're still wrestling with. If so, appendix C offers a number of ways to help you learn more about yourself.

Once you've come to a fair understanding of your abilities, the next step is to explore the workplace to see where your characteristics fit in. Or better yet, where you can create a niche.

This will be one time when you'll especially appreciate the research and analytical skills you picked up in college. Not only are they integral in most career-type jobs, but they're vital for researching a great new position. For instance, by analyzing your most remarkable traits and abilities and correlating them with specific industries, positions and companies will help you determine a career that's you! Are you patient? Do you like to instruct? Maybe you'd like to work with the handicapped, the elderly, small children? Do you feel strongly about working with the public? You might consider a sales position, customer service, personnel work. Or maybe you'd love a career that allows you to be creative. There are thousands available that draw upon new concepts, new products, designs and systems.

In fact, universities, businesses, public libraries, career centers and guidance offices all offer useful research on specific industries, positions and companies. Professional societies and trade associations also offer free or low-cost material on careers that might interest you and make use of your talents.

One of the most popular sources of career information, the *Occupational Outlook Handbook*, details a wide range of positions in industry today.[18] In addition it summarizes the educational and training requirements, advancement possibilities and earnings for each career. Take a look at some occupations they highlight under literary arts:

— journalist	— manuscript reader
— scriptwriter	— index editor
— advertising worker	— literary agent
— technical writer	— bookstore manager
— greeting card writer	— publisher's representative
— crossword puzzle writer	— book club sales associate
— public relations writer	

A less current publication, but one that could certainly help you pinpoint a career, is *What Can I Do With A Major In . . . ?* by Lawrence R. Malnig and Sandra L. Morrow. This book contains over 190 careers for many different majors. It's published by St. Peter's College Press.

There are a number of other sources — books, brochures, audio-visual materials — on occupations. Most of them should be in your local library. Although some of the data may overlap from source to source, each may touch on something specific that grabs you. Three

---

[18] *Occupational Outlook Handbook*, 1984–1985 edition (U.S. Bureau of Labor Statistics, Bulletin 2205), p. 2.

major references have been highlighted and described in Appendix D.

Before deciding on a specific career it helps to learn the basic structure of a company and how it functions. Companies in almost every field, from broadcasting to financial investment, have similar departments. So knowing the structure will bring you closer to making your career decision. Once you've narrowed your scope to a department and a few positions the next step will be to choose a field/industry where this position is found.

Take a close look at the organization chart at the top of page 90. It's a fairly basic overview of the pecking order within a firm. Naturally the chairman is the top banana. Underneath him is the company president, the person who answers directly to the chairman. Sometimes you will hear the term CEO (Chief Executive Officer). In some companies this is the chairman and in others it is the president. Reporting to the president, are the division vice presidents and so on down the line. Naturally, depending on the size of the company, some will have more divisions than pictured, others will have fewer. But this chart is suitable for our purposes. You'll also notice that under vice president accounting/ finance, and vice president sales, are a number of boxes. These too will vary with the type and size of the organization. The other areas headed by vice presidents have breakdowns of their own, but it's not necessary to go through each in detail. However, if we were to take a closer look at the subdivisions within, say, the sales division, it might look like the bottom chart on page 90. This shows the positions available in sales, and the ladder you'd have to climb to get to be the vice president.

Let's look at the responsibilities each division or department handles. As we go through the list write down those that appeal to you. Keep in mind that one person usually handles several responsibilities within a division and usually the most interesting are filled by people with more experience than recent graduates. That fact alone is one of the greatest catalysts that gets people working on their skills. After all, most career-seekers are eager to get promoted, and presumably, to reap the rewards of more responsibilities.

• **operations/manufacturing** — production control; quality assurance; purchasing; shipping; receiving; supplies; safety; security; cost control.

• **human resources division** — corporate personnel policies; job descriptions; annual job appraisals; recruitment; salary ranges; employee interactions/morale; benefits; labor relations; employee health and safety; training and development; staff planning; problem-solving.

• **data processing division** — MIS (management information systems); computer programming; application programming; system programming; tape library; security.

• **administration department** — office functions; correspondence; clerical duties; telephone communication; maintenance; office supplies; security.

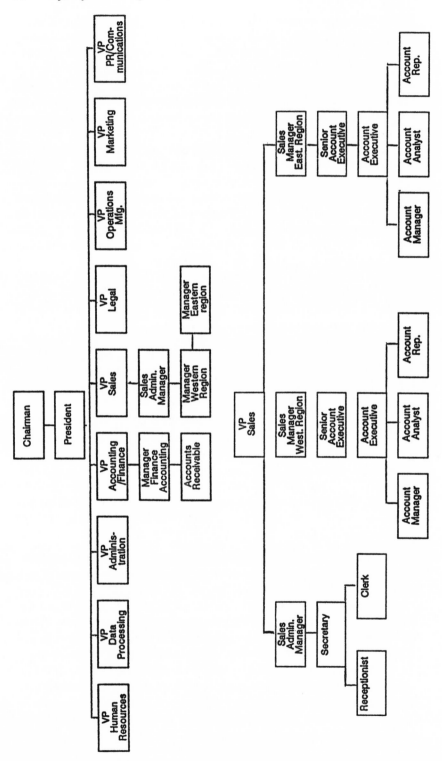

• **accounting/finance department** — maintains all corporate finances; investing; auditing and control; annual financial reports; accounting; payroll; tax management; planning/forecasting (annual, year-to-date and future revenues and goals); budgeting.

• **sales division** — generates revenue; generates new sales; maintains existing sales business; selling products and services; customer contact; client support/customer service; travel; negotiations.

• **legal department** — contract administration; mergers and acquisitions; patents; copyrights.

• **marketing division** — market research of supply and demand; product sampling and testing; telemarketing; advertising and promotion; creative services.

• **public relations/communications department** — community affairs; national customer relations; inter/intra industry relations; media interactions; government relations; corporate literature.

Think about what appeals to you, where you might fit in and what skills you can offer. Would you like more information? Is there a specific department that stands out? Or a responsibility that sounds interesting? If so, keep a list. Such a list will be important to refer to when you get to the part on information interviewing. It's discussed later in this chapter.

Now that you have the basic idea of the structure of a typical company and its divisions, the next step is to research some of the industries that appeal to you. Here is a list for reference. This naturally isn't complete but will help to narrow your focus:

— banking	— travel/leisure	— insurance
— real estate	— finance	— forestry
— mining	— agriculture	— law & government
— science	— fishing	— education
— religion	— engineering	— health & medicine
— petroleum	— publishing	— sports & recreation
— arts & entertainment	— computers/software	— social science

One group that has been omitted is one that includes unique jobs. It contains such fields as atomic energy, etymology, demographics and covers such positions as floriculturist, record album designer, and ultrasonographer. If you're especially interested in an unusual or exotic type of occupation, there are a number of publications on the subject.

A lot of glamour is usually associated with jobs considered unique so it's crucial to research the area before getting yourself too excited. Some extra facts can be all you'll need to wipe the romantic mist from your eyes and put matters into perspective. After all, many occupations that fall into this group can demand extra hours, involve an element of danger and can ask that you relocate away from friends or family. Nicholas comes to mind. He's worked for many years in a major fashion design house. Nicholas designs women's apparel, arranges fashion shows, selects fabrics and handles all the responsibilities of a top-notch designer. It's fascinating to see what he'll create next and to discuss styles with him. But a conversation with Nicholas doesn't happen frequently since he spends most of his time in Hong Kong and India.

Whether unique or not, occupations usually have their drawbacks as well as rewards. That's why it's so important to investigate the field, company and position you're interested in before you pursue it. Research the nature of the job: responsibilities, skills needed, equipment used, education required and lifestyle you're likely to have. Consider the size of the company. In most cases a job within a large corporation concentrates on a limited number of duties. One in a smaller firm, however, allows an employee to take on a wider variety of responsibilities.

When Mary left her account-executive position at a small brokerage company, she was set for all the knowledge, experience and contacts she'd gain at her new job. What she wasn't ready for, however, was the narrower range of tasks that were required. True, Mary will learn a lot in a larger firm, but her duties often seem repetitious.

Another important aspect to consider when deciding on a career is the working conditions. Are they suitable for your personality, habits, skills? Likewise, will you fit in the company's style? Some jobs offer a noisy environment, late hours, travel; while others practically demand that you dress a certain way, forfeit weekends, or work outdoors. Whether or not these conditions are a plus or minus really depends on you, your likes and desires. So it's a good idea to research a position thoroughly before striving for it.

Besides going to the library, reading source material and watching audio/visual programs, there's another very effective way to gather information about the career that interests you. It's a technique that will not only supply you with valuable information, but it will help establish contacts, confidence, and build important fact-finding skills. It's called *information interviewing.*

By setting an appointment with people in the fields, companies and positions that appeal to you and discussing important issues, needs and facts—you can gather vital information to help you make a career decision.

Information interviewing also gives you the opportunity to expose your interests and abilities to influential people in key spots. This is always beneficial since later on in your career the contacts you establish may be able to help you in other ways, or vice versa. Information interviewing is a method that not only helps you gather important first-hand facts, it builds contacts and confidence, and helps give you a competitive edge. Take a look at Appendix E for a step-by-step approach.

Job-Seeking Methods That Work!

Don't let anything negative you read or hear discourage you. Even though people refer to job-hunting as a full-time career, and just because some statistics show that the competition is tough, doesn't mean the search you're about to take on is hopeless. In fact, with the right combination of time, energy and job-seeking methods, you can make this year's job forecast even brighter than anticipated. According to a recent survey done by the College Placement Council, "During the past year, while the economy was picking up steam, the nation's college graduates were waiting to feel the effect. Well, the wait appears to be over. The job outlook for new college graduates is much better than it was a year ago..."[19]

Now that you're job-hunting you're probably also hearing a lot of controversy about which job-seeking method is best. Truth is, the ideal method is the one that helps you get the position you want. So for your first job perhaps networking will prove successful. Next time, the want ads and the next, maybe through an employment agency. That's why it's best to cover virtually all angles when you're ready to look for work. Of course, some methods are more highly recommended by experts than others. The reasons will be clear to see. But if you review practically all methods available and tailor-design a campaign using the most effective ones, then your outcome should be successful.

It took me one afternoon to get my first career-type job. Of course I had a lot more incentive than you'll probably have. I was awakened from a sound sleep by my mother who threatened to throw me out of the house unless I found work. (She was justified, I had been lazy.) So I grabbed the phone book, called every publisher listed, had an interview that afternoon and was offered the job that evening.

Although it has happened to others, I don't suspect job-hunting will be this easy for everyone. It certainly wasn't the next time I looked for work. But with the right combination of initiative, persistence, a good résumé, a cover letter and professional interviewing skills, you'll have a job-hunting strategy that will bring you closer to your goals. Here are some conventional job-finding techniques.

1) *Directly to Employer.* Because companies receive thousands of résumés each year, mass mailing yours to firms that interest you isn't considered the most favorable technique. In fact, in a survey done some years ago, it was estimated that for every 245 résumés received, one person was called for an interview.[20] That ratio can't be much better today.

If this kind of mass mailing still appeals to you, then there is a better approach, namely, by phone. Appendix F details the method explicitly. When you're ready to launch a telephone campaign to potential employers, refer to this section for specifics.

---

[19] "Job Outlook Brighter for New College Grads," News Release, College Placement Council, Inc. (July 25, 1984), p. 1.

[20] *Electronic Design 16* (New York: Deutsch, Shea & Evans Inc.), p. 63.

2) *Friends/Relatives.* Never underestimate the power of a connection. Although you may feel you can get a job on your own, a family member or friend can put you in touch with a key person in your field. Since no one will hire you solely because you have a mutual acquaintance, why not take advantage of an opportunity to bypass the personnel department (unless, of course, that's where you want to work)? Why not give yourself a chance to stand apart from the competition?

Tell the people around you that you're looking for work. Discuss your career objective and review your skills and qualifications. You never know what might happen.

It made Stewart's day to find out his older brother rode the train every day with a chemist for International Foods. So Stewart gave the chemist a call, introduced himself and followed all the professional tips he had read on job-hunting. After all, even though the chemist was his brother's buddy, Stewart still had to prove his professionalism. He met the chemist and discussed his plans, skills and goals. Stewart was offered a job.

3) *Want Ads.* Did you know that only 15% of all jobs available are advertised? That means 85% of all vacant positions are discovered in ways other than professional or trade journal ads, newspaper classifieds. Despite these statistics people still pore over the pages of their daily gazette with hopes of finding that great new position. And why not? Somebody's got to fill the opening.

Consulting classified ads is okay as long as you keep your search in perspective with the facts. For starters, competition between other job-hunters is very high; some employers hastily place ads only to discover the vacancy was never okayed by upper management. Other companies are compelled by corporate policy to advertise all available positions, even though the opening may have already been filled through some other method. And one of the most discouraging facts of all is that some professionals place classified ads to see who's available in the job-hunting marketplace. Or even worse than that, they do it to fatten the employment agency file.

It's true, answering an ad can certainly be a waste a time. But don't let that possibility discourage you. Many people find ideal positions this way. See Appendix G for guidance.

Now what about placing your own ad? Personal ads vary in cost, as well as in effect. Depending on the publication, they can run anywhere from one day or until you decide it's getting too expensive (which, by the way, may only be a day). And they can certainly seem like a desperate measure. Almost like the matrimonials that request "a companion, under 30, over 6′3″, who speaks Swahili and Cantonese." In other words, for recent college graduates, placing an ad is usually a waste of time and money. After all, employers don't have to go hunting for someone in a first-time career capacity. They can sit back and wait for you to track them down.

4) *Employment Agencies.* Thousands of employment agencies are in operation today and hundreds more open every year. All can be subdivided into four basic groups. Some you may be familiar with, others you may be hearing for the first time. Yet none is on the top of any expert's list for finding that initial career-type job. (Unless, of course, that list is being compiled by employment agency owners.) Let's look at each of the four types and investigate why.

Executive Search Firms. Otherwise known as headhunters, executive search firms deal with professionals who already know the kind of job they want and have quite a bit of solid experience in that field. Although executive search firms were traditionally associated with workers earning sizable amounts — close to or well above $100,000 a year — several are now handling young hopefuls in the $30–40,000 range.

Executive search firms are paid by companies who are seeking employees. These companies usually give search firms a percentage of the employee's first year salary. This is basically why headhunters seek out the outstanding professionals within an industry and place them in a higher paying position as quickly as possible. This type of firm is clearly something you should think about later on in your career, especially if you have highly marketable skills and very little time to job hunt.

Private Employment Agencies (free-of-charge & fee related). Although private employment agencies tend to specialize in one or several specific fields — accounting, marketing, banking, advertising, computers, etc. — all can be separated into two distinct categories: private employment agencies that offer their services to the job-seeker free-of-charge; and there are private employent agencies that charge the job-hunter.

The first agency mentioned, the kind that offers services free-of-charge, may sound like a real hot bargain. So let's take a closer look.

Since these agencies are paid by companies whose vacancies they fill, their main concern is not pleasing the job-seeker. They concentrate on the employer's needs since it's how they make money.

This can mean you won't be getting the kind of top-drawer service you might expect. For someone with limited career-related experience, an advisor might rush through an interview, handling you as a commodity rather than a person who wants a job. For candidates with more marketable experience, an advisor may over glamourize a position. Or he or she might send you on an interview for a job beneath your ability or only slightly related to your field.

Private employment agencies have a very high turnover of applicants. They may screen six or seven for one available opening, send two to the company for an interview and never see any of them again. And agencies of this sort have a tendency to deal mainly with lower level jobs.

After six years of copywriting experience and four months of job-hunting, Diedre decided to give an employment agency specializing in the arts a try. They welcomed her with a typing test, gave her a 20-minute interview and called her the next day for a temporary clerical job. This wouldn't have been unusual had Diedre asked to work in a clerical position, but she had specifically emphasized her desire to get a writing job. Is Diedre's case one in a million? Research on the subject claims not.

Employment agencies however, can be very helpful. If you'd like to give one a try, turn to Appendix H before making a move. It can save you a lot of time and aggravation.

Public Employment Service. One of the main reasons to use a public employment service would be to take advantage of the vocational testing programs each offers free-of-charge. As mentioned in a previous section, tests of this nature help determine a career that's right for you.

In addition, public employment services, which fall under the direction of the Labor Department's U.S. Employment Service, allow job seekers to examine a computerized listing of job openings. Staff members provide information on available positions, arrange for interviews, and provide a variety of services for special groups like veterans, people who speak little English, lack self-confidence, etc.

Although public employment services are designed to help all job-seekers, and are free-of-charge, recent college graduates are not the most popular group seen there. Apparently, a very low percentage of job-hunters find work through them and those who do, usually keep their jobs for a limited duration.

5) *Campus Career Development & Placement Centers.* Because it's a common trait to ignore a good thing when you have it, more and more colleges and universities are inviting graduates back. And for one very specific reason: to take advantage of the career development and placement services.

An increasing number of graduates is coming back for vocational testing, tips on job-hunting techniques, seminars on résumé writing, interviewing and more. Campuses are even offering listings for graduates to contact alumni in the same field.

Although these services are offered to undergraduates free-of-charge, schools are now asking graduates to pay a nominal fee. Why not look into your alma mater?

6) *Networking.* It's a term you'll certainly hear more often now that you're entering the professional arena. And one that should definitely become a part of your life. Networking is a system used throughout the business community to spread information, ideas and concepts — as well as to link its participants to unadvertised job openings. (Unpublished vacancies amount to 85 percent of what's available.)

Now that you've decided to seek a position in a particular field, one of the ways to attain that position, and grow within that industry, is to establish relationships with individuals who are already involved. From newcomers to opinion leaders, formal acquaintances to casual friends, everyday companions to once-in-a-lifetime contacts, the people you know and keep in touch with will not only inform you of the latest industry news, but will help you become and stay visible.

There are many ways to get yourself involved in a network that you can gain from. One way is to join existing professional organizations, clubs or associations within the field you've chosen. This will give you the opportunity to mingle with members in all facets of the field, exchange ideas and learn from them. For more information on such associations, consult the *Encyclopedia of Associations* published by Gale Research Co.

Professionals are even setting up formal networks. One such group named the "Good Old Girls"[21] was organized a few years ago. It represents over 2,400 career-oriented women. For dues ranging from $5–$100 annually, this affiliation provides seminars on topics such as speech writing, job stress, and managerial techniques, as well as providing an avenue to discover job vacancies. The "Good Old Girls" is one of many groups of this kind. Others can be investigated by reading professional and trade journals, and industry newsletters.

Networks are something you can initiate too. By using your imagination and being assertive, you can set up your own channels of communication. First of all, keep in touch with influential people you may have already met through school. Certainly many of your professors are good contacts, as are the people you might have encountered through seminars and campus career programs. Why not visit them or call to talk about the industry, its people, events, openings?

In addition, any department heads, managers, family friends or relatives you may have interviewed for information are also great sources. Keep them informed of your new plans and career goals and ask them and their contacts for an interview. For a quick review on techiques, re-read the section on information interviewing in Appendix E.

Speaking of information interviewing, you can also make some cold calls to key professionals you've read about, wanted to meet, or would enjoy discussing industry trends, opinions and issues with. Very likely they will have a friend who has a neighbor who has a vacancy.

Certainly one of the best networks to set up is keeping in touch with ex-coworkers in key positions. Whether they move to another company or position, or whether you move, maintaining your relationship, even if it's a once-a-month phone call, is a fantastic way to cull facts and keep visible.

Networking is a system that takes time to develop and a skill that is perfected through your imagination and assertiveness. Now is the time to start forming and joining industry channels so that you can learn, discover and find that great new job.

---

[21] "Old Girls and Old Boys," *Time Magazine*, 26 Oct. 1981, p. 68.

7) *Other Techniques.* Job-seeking is an art that draws upon your initiative, knowledge and imagination. The most popular methods have been discussed, but surely the list is not complete. Many job-seekers have resorted to rather zany tactics for getting work, at times with success.

Brian had a very disappointing day job-hunting until he stopped for a red light just blocks from his home. In front of him was a car whose license plate read "AD MAKER." Without a second thought, Brian leaped out of the car and handed the driver his résumé. Perhaps the nature of the advertising business creates professionals who recognize quick-acting, hard-hitting actions of this sort. But not all will be as accepting as the "ad maker" who called Brian the next day for an interview, especially because methods like this tend to appear desperate. Like Maggie's. She drove through the corporate parking lot and attached her résumé to the windshields of all cars parked in spaces reserved for top management. Or Tom's. He marched right into the president's office and announced why he was the perfect candidate for the job. Would you want someone that brazen and unprofessional working for you?

One of my favorites was the technique my husband used some years ago. He knew how unhappy I was with my job, so when I came back from an interview even more discouraged, he took action. He called every publisher listed in the yellow pages and asked to speak to the marketing director. His sales pitch went like this:

"Hello Mr./Ms. —————. I'm calling from the White Plains Employment Agency. I've just interviewed a young copywriter..." He described my skills, the position I was looking for and the salary range I wanted. That afternoon I had three appointments for interviews.

Believe me, I'm not advocating forming a fictitious employment agency to get work. Nor am I condemning any way-out methods to find a job. I simply want to illustrate that very unconventional methods can be used with care. Recognize, however, that not many will be successful. While some industries tend to be more flexible than others few are interested in obnoxious job-seekers who appear desperate.

Two Final Points. Keep a running tally of whom you contacted, the date, time, company and outcome. This will avoid duplicate calls, wasted postage or an untimely appointment. When I headed the advertising department for a small direct mail company, I often got calls asking for interviews. One in particular I remember was from a character who read an introduction to me in a monotone voice, then insisted I interview him. Don't ask me what type of job he wanted, his conversation was too dull. I politely told him there were no openings and suggested he try a larger firm. That afternoon he phoned with the same monologue. Two days later he called again. Being persistent is one thing, being disorganized is another. Even if a job had been available, I wouldn't have interviewed that scatterbrain.

Speaking of persistence, you'll need plenty of it. Not only for that first career-type job, but throughout your years job-hunting. All too often, job-seekers start their campaign enthusiastic and full of vigor. Then, after a few negative responses, perhaps a bad interview, they are pessimistic and blue. This is a normal reaction. The ideal position won't always be waiting for you when you're ready to look. Nor will you always be the ideal candidate for a job you're dying to get. If you find the job hunt is getting you down...watch an old movie. Read a book. Buy something. And work on maintaining your self-esteem.

The Resume

Contrary to what you might think, a résumé won't get you a job. Although employers place a lot of emphasis on how a résumé is presented and what it says, it's only one of many tools they use to choose the perfect candidate for their opening. A résumé tells them who you are, the position you want, your experience, skills and education. It's an introduction whose purpose is to get you an interview.

Résumés come in a variety of shapes and sizes, colors and formats. Some job-seekers think an unusual eye-catcher will help them stand out and improve their chances of getting a job. The truth is, an employer wants to get acquainted with each hopeful by glancing quickly down a page of details. Bob Yardis, Personnel Director at Pergamon Press, Inc., says, "Employers are too busy to wade through long résumés that go on and on about nothing important...they want to see the facts 1, 2, 3 clearly, concisely and with no typos please." So even though a résumé won't secure a job for you — a poor résumé can ruin your chances of becoming a candidate.

That's why successful job-seekers tend to shy away from gimmicky types of résumés and play it safe by using a format that's easy to read and appealing to the eye. To introduce themselves, some use a functional format, others a chronological one. Let's look at these in detail and see how each fares in the marketplace.

A *functional résumé* highlights a job-seeker's skills by listing them in broad headings and supporting each with facts. To prepare a functional résumé a person must review his or her past accomplishments, training, experience and qualities — and focus specifically on those that correlate to the position desired. See the example of a functional résumé on page 100.

Whichever program of job-hunting techniques Phillip designs, he has a résumé tailored to the position, field and type of company he'd like to work for. Each skill is supported by relevant part-time experience, as well as extra-curricular activities. However, the résumé style Phillip has chosen, the *functional kind*, is not the most popular one nor the one most preferred. Résumés of this type are vague and tend to hide lack of experience or job gaps. For the new job-seeker who has very little experience, perhaps this is the only resort. But it's one that

PHILLIP RYAN
1718 Sylvan Road
Havertown, PA 10983
(215) 555-1285

CAREER OBJECTIVE
Product Manager for sporting goods/recreational equipment
firm.

FIELD KNOWLEDGE
Thorough awareness of most sporting goods and recreational
equipment including competitive brands, product lines,
usage, market prices. Gathered knowledge from five-year
employment at Wayside Sporting Goods, Inc.

PROBLEM-SOLVING ABILITY
Remedied customer complaints. Identified employee problems
and implemented changes in scheduling system.

LEADERSHIP/INITIATIVE
Part-time manager for sporting goods firm. Promoted from
cashier. Coached little league baseball team for Havertown
Youth Program.

CREATIVITY
Displayed and often ordered new recreational equipment and
product lines.

EDUCATION
B.S. in Marketing from the University of Ohio.

RELATIVE PERSONAL SKILLS
Yankee farm team recruit. Knowledge of all sports.

REFERENCES
Will be furnished on request.

can certainly be avoided by increasing skills, work-related experience (no matter how little) and with some good, hard facts.

A common error many recent graduates make is to leave out traits and experience that relate to the position they want. When it comes time to write a résumé, they sometimes overlook important features or put aside their part-time work experience as if it had no relevance. Often there are key qualities in your past that can make you a more outstanding candidate. "One of the reasons my first employer hired me was that I had written I was an Eagle Scout on my résumé," says Mike Crawford of Babich & Associates, an employment agency in Dallas. "Being an Eagle Scout told him that when all the other kids were out goofing around, I was developing characteristics and initiative by earning merit badges."

By carefully reviewing your past you may be able to gather relevant characteristics too. Are you overlooking the fact that you are creative? Able to work with details? A good team player? Are you competitive? Do your part-time/volunteer efforts show you have initiative, motivation, leadership abilities? Qualities like these will help you gain a competitive edge over other job-seekers. And because some you learned on-the-job, you'll be able to arrange them in a résumé format most favorably accepted in the marketplace: namely the chronological one.

The chronological résumé has almost all the same features as a functional one: name, address, phone, career objective, education, personal traits. The only difference is the middle section. Instead of listing major groups of skills, the chronological résumé lists work experience in order of occurrence. From the last position filled, on down, it features position, company, dates employed, tasks performed, accomplishments. Of course, not all your part-time, summer help or volunteer jobs will be applicable, but usually the most recent ones will highlight your most marketable qualities.

A good way to start writing a résumé of this type is to jot down every job you've held, every internship you completed and any volunteer work you took on. Analyze the list you've compiled while writing down all duties you performed, any promotions you received, any merit awards earned.

If you've already written a brief biography (Appendix C asks for one) then it's smart to refer to that. It'll help you position your skills, abilities and experience in a way that will be appealing to employers. Appendix I features an example of a chronological résumé written by a recent graduate who doesn't have too much experience in the field she wants to pursue. She does, however, certainly know how to get noticed.

It's sometimes difficult to teach someone how to make him or herself appear as marketable as possible. But when you're ready to compose that award-winning résumé, appendix I will provide ideas and tips that will give you that important edge.

Your résumé is an introduction to you. It should represent you in

Philip Ryan
1718 Sylvan Road
Havertown, PA 19083
(215) 555-1285

Career Objective

Product Manager for a sporting goods/recreational equipment firm.

Experience

1980-1985   Wayside Sporting Goods, Inc.
            Havertown, PA

Manager: Summer manager for branch of sporting goods
            retail chain. Displayed and often ordered new
            recreational equipment and product lines. As a
            result, have thorough awareness of most sporting
            goods and recreational equipment including
            competitive brands, product lines usage, market
            prices. Identified employee problems and
            implemented changes in scheduling system.
            Promoted to summer manager after one year as
            part-time cashier.

Education

University of Ohio, Cincinnati, Ohio
Bachelor of Science: Marketing Major
Graduated May, 1987

Related Interests

Yankee farm team recruit. Knowledge of all sports. Coached little league baseball team for Havertown Youth Program 1980-1982.

Reference

Will be furnished on request.

the best possible light and should be written in a chronological format. If this is totally impossible perhaps you should work on boosting your background. Take some career-related seminars, join associations, volunteer within the field or take a lower level job or internship. By acquiring a few more supporting qualifications it will be almost impossible for you to avoid the chronological format. Without adding anything extra, let's rewrite Phillip's résumé as shown on page 102.

The Cover Letter

A cover letter should accompany any résumé. Whether you're sending yours to a friend in the business, mailing it out cold or responding to an ad, a cover letter should be attached to the top of the résumé before you insert it in the envelope. The cover letter should state briefly the career you want, skills you can offer, how you obtained the person's name, and how he or she can reach you.

The cover letter should be neatly typed on a 8½" × 11" page. It must be written professionally, in business letter format and it must be grammatically correct, error free and contain the correct name, title, company name and address of the person you are writing to. Two samples for reference can be found in Appendix J.

The Envelope

It seems almost ridiculous to discuss the envelope but there have been some real lulus written in our day. My favorite looked like this, the envelope sample at the top of page 104.

Was this person writing to the lonely hearts department? Naturally it should have read Personnel Department.

The envelope is easy to address, yet very important. First of all, use a #10 envelope. It's a legal size which measures 4⅛" × 9½". Type your name and address in the upper left hand corner, then the name, title, company name and address you're writing to, in the center of the envelope. If you prefer, write to the company and send it to the attention of a specific person, then complete it as shown in the example at the bottom of page 104. The envelope should be white and typed in black ink.

"Thanks But No Thanks"

I call them "Thanks But No Thanks" letters. They're the negative responses you receive from a company you may have called, sent a résumé to, interviewed with or all of these. They're letters that can be as impersonal as those written on a computer or as vague as those that tell you they love your qualifications, but they can't fit you in. The nerve!

No matter how disappointing rejection letters may be, don't let them discourage you. Every one gets them at one time or another. And most people don't think twice about them. It's just something you learn to accept as part of the whole job-hunting process. The one shown on page 106 illustrates my point.

Mr. H. Looluk
1314 Smith Road
Vestavia Hills, AL 35202

                          Palmetto Publishing
                          23 Sunrise St.
                          Mountain Brook, AL 35223

Attn: <u>Personal</u> Dept.

Ms. G. Yatt
82 Longview Avenue
Wallingford, WA 98103

                          Heathcote & Sons, Inc.
                          1685 North Court, Ste. 13D
                          Rivertown, WA 98107

Attn: Ms. Genie Teran
      Computer Services Division

The Interview

Being interviewed is like selling a product — you have to package yourself effectively. That includes highlighting your skills appropriately, asking pertinent questions, behaving professionally and dressing accordingly. Dean Toby A. Hale of Wake Forest University says, "The working world won't be nearly as forgiving of your lack of preparation as the academic world may be." That's why it's imperative to know what to expect and how to position yourself. It can mean the difference between an interview that's wishy-washy and one that's clearly a winner! For a complete run down of what to wear, expect, ask and answer, during and after the interview, appendices K and L provide important information.

Job seekers frequently misunderstand the purpose of a job interview. They don't realize a job-seeker is actually interviewing the employer at the same time the employer is interviewing the job-seeker. Although an employer may find you to be the perfect candidate for the job, it may be a job that isn't right for you. So take advantage of the interview situation and screen the interviewer too. Not only will you gather important facts to help you make a career decision, but you will appear more assertive, aware and interested.

Which Offer Is Right?

The hard part is over. You've determined the field and position you want to work in. You've gone on interviews and have been offered a job. But is the company right for you? Although your impulse may be to jump at the first job offered, there are a few additional factors to consider about the company itself.

Is the location suitable? Whether you're relocating or traveling two miles from home, evaluate the company aesthetically. Will you work in a smoke-filled, crowded atmosphere? Or will you have a private office? Will the neighboring vicinity meet your needs? What about the shops available, community services, restaurants and other personal services? Consider the geography, travel conditions and how they'll affect you. Liz took a job at the only office park in a rural community. Although she has her own office and loves to take nature walks at lunch, the locale has its drawbacks. Every time Liz has to get to the dry cleaners, she packs a lunch, drives seven miles and eats during the trip. This may be a complete turn-off to some. To Liz, it's worth the occasional inconvenience.

The Chamber of Commerce can be a great help. If you're concerned about an area, they have information on hand, detailing demographic research, community services, housing, banking, transportation, educational and recreational facilities. Why not give them a call?

Another factor to consider before giving a potential employer the "okay" is coworkers. Some you may have met during your interviews. Others you might have seen in passing. Even though any judgment will

SYSTEMS DESIGNS, 122 Main Street, Belleville, IL 62222

August 18, 1987

Mr. Edward Colungo
36 Maplemore Street
Belleville, IL 62223

Dear Mr. Colungo:

Thank you for your interest in employment with Systems
Designs.

After a thorough review of your qualifications, we are
unable to identify a position which would utilize your
experience to our mutual advantage.

My inability to give you a more favorable reply does not
indicate a negative view of your qualifications; rather it
is an indication of the intense competition for the limited
openings available.

I regret that my response cannot be more encouraging and
wish you success in locating a challenging and rewarding
opportunity.

Sincerely,

P.R. Rondo
Director of Personnel

have to be a superficial one, the people you came in contact with must have left an impression. Do they look like people you can relate to? Of course, it's difficult to tell for certain, but you can usually get a general idea if you will fit in. Notice the way people dress, the size of the company and the general employee age.

Jack knew immediately the job was for him. It was a mid-sized company that hired a healthy cross-section of age groups. This is not to say Jack was looking for a potential confidante. The point is, when you're fresh out of college, you don't want to spend eight hours a day, five days a week in a predicament like Laura's. Her first job was in a room packed with desks arranged in neat little clusters. All but one employee was a smoking male over 40. The other one was a woman who had three front teeth and painted eyebrows.

Salary is always an important factor to think about, but don't let it override your goals. If a company has terrific growth potential but pays $3,000 less than another option, consider the implications. Is an additional $57 dollars a week worth risking the chance to be promoted? Then again you can always negotiate with the lower paying company so that you won't have to sacrifice a larger salary. But remember the less workplace experience you have the less bargaining power you have.

Speaking of growth potential, what other opportunities does the company offer? Are formal training programs available? Seminars? Will you learn from the higher-ups? If you're a self-starter will you have the freedom to take charge of your own responsibilities? Or does it seem like you'll be spoon-fed by a threatened supervisor?

What about fringe benefits? You've probably heard stories about a person employed by a record company who gets free albums. Another who manages a boutique and gets a store discount. Company benefits can certainly be enticing but they are usually fairly basic in entry level, career-type jobs. It's true that they vary from company to company so consider the ones that will affect you most when selecting a job. Think about medical coverage, disability and profit-sharing. The chart on page 108 can help you evaluate what a potential employer has available.

The above plans are very good. Many companies offer some, but not all of these benefits. A few offer more.

Being patient is not always easy, especially when it comes to job-hunting. Money, self-esteem and disappointment may make you more eager to take a job you normally wouldn't consider. So try to take your time, review your goals and evaluate your options carefully.

How Good Are Your Benefits?

Health

What does it cost for coverage?

A Good Plan

charges very little or no insurance premium to the employee.

What does it cover?

covers fully paid hospital stays at least 21 days, diagnostic hospital admissions, mental health care, extended care facilities, visual care, dental care (including orthodontics and bridgework) and post retirement costs.

How big a deduction does it require on major medical?

requires less than $100 per individual and $300 per family for major medical, $50 and $150 for dental.

How much does it pay?

pays 80% of major medical and dental, 50% of mental health.

Disability

How much does it pay for short-term disability?

pays full salary depending on the length of service, and half salary thereafter up to six months.

What about long term disability?

pays 50% to 60% of final salary, offset by social security disability payments.

Profit Sharing and Thrift Plans

How much can you contribute?

lets you put up to 10% of your salary in the fund.

How much does company contribute?

matches at least $.50 per dollar of employee contribution. If it's a straight profit-sharing plan without employee contribution, a good plan contributes 2% to 3% of each employee's salary.

How easy are withdrawals?

permits withdrawals without imposing penalties

How is the plan vested?

vests 100% within 5 or 6 years.

Does it replace a pension plan?

definitely doesn't substitute for a pension plan, it supplements it. [22]

---

[22] "How to Size Up Your Company Fringe Benefits," *Business Week*, 12 May 1980, p. 136.

THE NON-CAREER
RELATED JOB.

Why take a menial job when you could begin a career? Even the most mundane position can be rewarding if a person uses it to his or her advantage. For starters, waitressing, house repairs, domestic work are terrific ways to earn a decent income while creating your own work schedule. The extra time you have for yourself can be devoted to the career you'd like to start. Many artsy types can be found in the kitchens of the dingiest restaurants in town. They may not be crazy about slinging hash or carting greasy plates, but when their shift is through, not only do they have a pocket filled with money (so maybe it *is* all change), but they have a good portion of the day to spend on their craft. Take Tom. He's probably the most talented baritone who ever served me chili. And until he breaks into show business he'll probably stay that way. And why not? He has time for voice lessons, acting school and auditions all before he starts his dinner shift.

Of course, if you're not as directed as Tom, driving a cab, answering phones, painting houses are ideal jobs until you decide what you really want to do. There's nothing wrong with taking some time to think over your options — as long as you have a specific plan to stick to, that includes doing plenty of research. Besides, work of this sort has driven many a college graduate to speed up his decision-making process. After all, how many envelopes can you address before you go totally bonkers?

"Chimpanzee work," as my waitressing buddies used to call it, supports thousands of people who want to continue their studies. It keeps millions afloat until their "real" careers finally pan out. And it provides self-starters with the necessary capital to start a business of their own. This reminds me of George. As soon as he graduated from college he took a truck-driving job. His parents had a lot to say about his work until he opened his own restaurant. Sure, now they're proud of ole Georgey-boy. It's just too bad they weren't as supportive while he was saving for the down payment.

Then again, if you're unsure which career you want, a short term, entry-level job can help. A position in each of the fields that interest you will certainly make a decision easier. That is, providing you do enough research while employed at each place.

Or maybe you're regretting that internship you never took. An entry-level position will give you the kind of job-related experience employers like to see. Joan L. Bloss has edited a book on internships published by Writer's Digest Books, Cincinnati, OH. It lists over 16,000 on-the-job training opportunities for all types of careers: from business and industry to cultural organizations, science / research to advertising. Maybe you should look into this option. You never know where an internship can lead. Look at Tracey. Just before she graduated, she was offered a permanent position at the ad agency where she did her internship. Most other people would have jumped at this opportunity, but Tracey's experience at the agency was all she needed to decide to go into real estate, which, by the way, was another interest of hers.

Whether you're on your way to Hollywood or still floundering between office parks, non-career related jobs, when manipulated correctly, can help you reach your goals. So the next time you pity the freezing toll taker, keep in mind that he may be about to earn a PhD in thermal engineering.

Prerequisites

It's an unusual situation but if you've never had a job of any kind, the first thing you'll need is a social security card and number. Appendix M will provide step-by-step instructions on how to get one.

Before applying for a job, as opposed to getting career work, it's important to consider the days and hours you are available. Jobs pumping gas, short order cooking, ringing up merchandise, are ones that aren't restricted to office hours (9 A.M. to 5 P.M.; 8:30 A.M. to 4:30 P.M.) or weekdays. So your work schedule can be flexible but within reason. After all, not many employers will hire a person to work one day a week, for three hours. If that's what you're looking for perhaps an office temp place is for you.

Before approaching the job scene determine whether you're willing to work weekends. Think about when you can start. And if you want to work nights. No one will be interested in a wishy-washy job applicant who hasn't decided any of these.

Jobs are certainly not as tough to get as career-work, but they can be obtained through similar methods. Some of the easiest ways are by word of mouth, through friends and relatives, newspaper ads, and by going to the place of business and filling out an application.

If your search involves making an unscheduled visit to a company, avoid their peak hours. For example, the worst time you can look for restaurant work is at mealtime. It's better to go either before eleven or after three in the afternoon. If you're not sure which are peak hours, call the establishment and ask the manager when it's convenient to apply for work — and be sure to identify yourself. The fact that you were considerate and conscientious will say a lot about your personality.

Suppose you're looking for a sales position. Ask to speak to the store manager, shake his or her hand, introduce yourself and say you're interested in a job selling. The more specific you are about the type of work you want, the better. If you don't know what kind of service you can offer an employer, he may find something unpleasant for you to do. I'll never forget the restaurant manager who hired me for one specific reason: to scrub the walk-in refrigerator for the day. If I didn't need the money so badly, I would have refused. Instead my day ended like a scene from the *I Love Lucy* TV show. I was cold, sneezing, had a stiff neck and drove home crying. So do yourself a favor and determine the skills you can offer an employer before you fill out an application.

If you call for, say, a waitressing job you saw listed in the newspaper, use an introduction like this: "Hello, my name is ————. I'm calling in reference to your ad in the *Sunday News* for a waitress. Can you tell me a little bit about the restaurant and the hours you need to fill?" If it sounds interesting, set up an appointment to meet the employer and to fill out an employment application.

If you're making a cold call to an establishment, find out the manager's name by asking the person who answered the phone. Then say something to this effect: "Hello, Mr./Ms. ————. My name is ————. I'm interested in a job ————. Do you have any openings?" If the answer is yes then schedule a time when you can meet and discuss the job. If no, ask if it would be worth your time to come in and fill out an application.

And finally, if a friend or relative knows an employer who needs help, call and ask to speak to him/her by name. Introduce yourself and mention the person who informed you of the opening. Tell the manager you're interested in a job and would like to meet him or her and fill out an application.

It's really very easy to get a job. The trick is to try each of these approaches until you find work. Each of them has been successful for me at one time or another. And as a result, I've probably served more hamburgers in my day than McDonalds. Of course, these approaches should be used for non-career related jobs only, since these employers aren't as particular as those you'll find when seeking career-type work.

Be prepared for an interview when you go to fill out an application. Jobs of this nature are usually filled quickly and as soon as possible. Gauge the type of outfit you should wear by the kind of company you are applying to and the kind of work you're seeking. Jobs like construction work, dish washing, counter help, certainly don't require a three-piece suit. So dress casually, but conservatively. Jeans, sneakers, trendy styles are fine after hours but on an interview they can be a turn-off. Janet lost out on a pretty lucrative job because the employer was squeamish about the extra holes she had pierced in her ears. So maybe it was "in" that year, but she should have left the extra earrings home. Don't misunderstand. You don't have to call your local nerd and ask to borrow clothes for the day. But if your hair is purple maybe you can get it back to its normal color before you look for work.

Make sure you are well-groomed. Don't chew gum, and smoke only when invited or if the interviewer lights a cigarette for himself. Be well-mannered, cooperative, alert and enthusiastic. Answer questions honestly. Use correct English and don't be afraid to ask particulars. Be prepared to talk about yourself, the jobs you've had, the things that interest you, your qualifications and the position you want.

For this type of work it's not necessary to go into a long dissertation on the do's and don't's of getting a job. But if you still feel uneasy about how to handle an interview, review the section in careers. Yours may not be as involved as that, but it will certainly help prepare you.

The Employment Application
Never underestimate the power of an employment application. It's a prerequisite to getting jobs of all kinds. And it's one of the deciding factors on whether or not a position is yours. From part-time clerical work to full-time computer programming, employers rely on application forms to learn more about you.

People seeking non-career related jobs, often rush through a form thinking their employer doesn't have to be impressed by credentials. Others decide they'd rather put their all into the interview. And those that come equipped with résumés ready to move up the corporate ladder sometimes look at these forms as degrading, not to mention a waste of time. Truth is, employers scrutinize employment applications seriously. These forms tell them who you are, where you live, what you've studied. Each shows many basic facts like date of birth, year of graduation, former employment. And each reveals a number of underlying qualities. For instance, a disorganized application, written illegibly, will give a potential employer a good idea of your work habits.

So employment applications are certainly a serious consideration when job hunting. For the applicant, they can mean the difference between getting an interview or being tossed aside. That's why it's especially important to be well-prepared when you go to fill one out. Having the necessary information available will not only speed up the process of completing one, but it will help you assemble facts in a way that will sell you best. See Appendix N for sample questions usually found on an employment application.

Forms
The employment application is only the beginning. Throughout your working years, as well as throughout your entire life, forms will be an integral part. From buying a car to selling a house, from medical claims to life insurance, the list of forms and applications is endless. In fact, a growing business within industry today is designing and printing special forms. While each is different, most ask similar questions and all provide a specific function that can sometimes drastically

affect our lives. How many people do you know have been denied financial aid because their forms were improperly filled? This is only one example of how an inaccurate or incomplete form can haunt you. That's why it's so important to take every application seriously, as well as to take the necessary time to complete one correctly.

Let's use the W-4 as an example. One of the first forms you'll be asked to complete once you're hired is the W-4, Employer's Withholding Allowance Certificate. It determines the amount of tax to be withheld from each individual's paycheck. Although this is a federal form, your payroll department will use it as a guide to withholding state tax too, if applicable. All too often, though, when new employees are asked to complete one, they either rush through it carelessly, or ask a non-professional for help. This is nothing unusual, especially since at first glance, the form seems pretty intimidating. But step-by-step directions are provided. If you're still confused after reading them it's a good idea to ask a staff accountant or friend within the field. After all, a mistake on the W-4 can certainly have its drawbacks.

1) the government can end up owing you a sizable amount of money. This isn't too bad except that you could've been using that extra money all year or perhaps could've been collecting interest on it if you had invested some.

2) you may find that you owe the government money. For some this can be a hardship.

Do yourself a favor: read forms carefully and answer them correctly. Although some seem pretty standardized, the answers to them are not. Responses can vary from time to time and from person to person.

Leaving A Job
It doesn't matter how angry you may be, it's better to leave a job professionally than by screaming and kicking. Although etiquette for resignation varies, it's wise to give an employer two weeks' notice. This will usually allow ample time to get a replacement.

However, there may be cases when a two-week delay will jeopardize your new endeavor. If this is so, the issue should be weighed according to how it affects your goals. There may be a time when you feel your employer won't be able to survive without you. But don't let your ego go haywire. It could be that a boss will miss you temporarily, but it's a cold, cruel fact that he'll bounce back quickly. And sometimes too quickly for your self esteem to handle.

In a non-career related job it's not necessary to go through a formalized process of resignation. Simply discussing your plans with your superior, in a positive manner, usually results in congratulations.

In a more corporate-type position, however, not only will you have to talk over your plans with your superior, but a memo of departure may be required. If this is the case you should write it clearly, succinctly and devoid of any type of emotion, as illustrated on page 114.

C. Unison, 123 Main St., Seattle, WA 98001

October 27, 1987

Mr. John Matheson, Manager
Eastern Region
Sales Division
Medi-Treatment Pharmaceuticals
1321 2nd Avenue
Seattle, WA 98001

Dear John:

Please accept my resignation effective November 10, 1987 as
Junior Sales Representative for Medi-Treatment
Pharmaceuticals. I am accepting a position with another
pharmaceutical firm that will allow me to stay in the
Seattle area.

Thank you for the knowledge and guidance I have received at
Medi-treatment and the best of luck to you and the company.

Sincerely,

Craig Unison
Junior Sales Representative

cc: Stewart Annetti, VP, Sales Division

HELP OTHERS WHILE YOU HELP YOURSELF.

Getting absorbed in your own affairs is a syndrome that's especially easy to succumb to, now that you've graduated from college. It starts with questions like: Will I get accepted into law school? Will I be offered the job I want? Can I earn enough money to travel? Then it evolves to issues concerning marriage, family, investments and more.

Every once in a while, though, we're reminded that there's more to life than what I can do for me. There is, in fact, a whole world outside that can use our help.

The hit single, "We Are the World," by USA for Africa, is one such reminder. Although you don't have to look too hard to find hunger, poverty, drug and alcohol abuse, crime, physical and emotional diseases — unless we are reminded that these problems exist — we somehow become oblivious to them. We simply assume someone else is taking care of them.

While hundreds even thousands of people work each day to meet many of our nation's needs, as well as the needs of other countries, the truth remains that more aid is necessary.

That's why volunteering is so important. Whether it's for one hour a year or eight hours a day, donating time and energy can mean progress. No matter what age you are, what sex or religion, no matter how much talent or money you have (or don't have), everyone has something to offer. And not only can the effort you contribute help others in an effective way, it can help you as a recent graduate too!

Volunteering May Lead to a Job

Volunteering is one way to get your foot in the door. In New York City, many graduates anxious to enter the television industry volunteer at Channel 13, a public supported station. By donating time to answer phone calls that pledge monetary support, individuals meet contacts, gain exposure and have a significant extra to display on their résumés. In fact, if a volunteer job specifically relates to a career you're pursuing, be sure to spell out specific skills you've acquired from the experience, on your résumé and during your interviews. Also be sure to illustrate what you've done by collecting samples, any awards or certificates of recognition, as well as any letters of recommendation from superiors.

Meeting People

For those of you who are moving back home or to a new area, volunteering is a great way to meet people, make contacts and learn about your community while offering valuable assistance. Not only can you make an important difference where you live, but where you live can become more rewarding to you. In most communities across the country, a volunteer service bureau is set up that will interview you and analyze your skills, talents and interests in order to place you in a suitable position. Consult the phone directory for the bureau nearest you.

Decide What You Want

If you're unsure what field you'd like to work in or study further, volunteering is yet another way to explore an industry that interests you. I was a communications major who wasn't committed to any specific area of the field. I had thought that radio was the direction I'd head in until I volunteered one summer at a local station. That was all I needed to see that, in fact, broadcast wasn't for me. I did, however, lend a hand, while picking up important skills that created opportunities for me to get what I wanted later on.

Likewise volunteering is a terrific way to explore a career change. During research for this book I came across a statistic that said most people change careers every four years. If the four-year-itch gets you later in life, donating some of your time is a safe step to take before you alter your entire line of work.

Volunteers are always in high demand; many resources are available to get people placed. Some are listed in the Appendix O. In addition to the agencies mentioned, many of the most prominent companies in this country are getting into the act too. Besides offering financial support, many now have programs where a small number of employees volunteer on company time. For instance, some firms match a volunteer's efforts hour by hour. That means for every hour a person donates his own energies, the company will allow him to volunteer an hour during office time. Some corporations allow employees to schedule their work day around volunteer commitments. These workers are free to begin their paying job between 8 A.M. and 10 A.M. and to regulate lunch and quitting time accordingly, as long as the work week consists of 35 hours in five days. Other firms go a step further by offering a limited number of employees paid leaves of absence (some as much as 6 months) so that they can complete a community project. During this time, workers draw full pay and benefits, and are guaranteed their jobs when they return.

If the company you'll work for doesn't offer one of these very generous programs, check to see if they'll reimburse you for travel expenses.

Many of the smaller banks, manufacturing firms, utility companies, etc., do their share to encourage employees to volunteer by paying for gas, tolls, and out-of-pocket expenses to and from the volunteer job.

Sharing and caring is what volunteering is all about. By taking it upon ourselves to lend a hand, we can improve the quality of life for others as well as for ourselves. Volunteering is a way to stay active and involved, have fun, become self-satisfied and, most importantly, make this world a better place to live.

Here are categories and positions you can fill:

1) HEALTH CARE

Types of Programs:	Responsibilities:
hospitals — physical / mental care	be a friendly visitor
hospice programs	assist in physical therapy
day treatment centers	do crisis intervention
institutes for the deaf / blind	provide library service
mental health centers	aid in blood donation
disaster programs	write letters
visiting health services	teach nutrition
veterans programs	comfort the terminally ill
public health clinics	advocate
national health organizations	speak on health subjects
counseling centers	take blood pressure
nursing homes	entertain
rehabilitation programs	drive
hotlines	do research
independent living centers	escort patients
drug / alcohol abuse centers	sell in a gift shop
programs for the homebound	interpret
halfway houses	work in the emergency room
nutrition programs	deliver meals
blood banks	drive an ambulance

2) HUMAN SERVICES

Types of Programs:	Responsibilities:
welfare centers	counsel
senior centers	escort
rehabilitation programs	research
abused women's programs	serve as a receptionist
self-help groups	assist with food service
veterans groups	read to the blind
friendly visiting programs	offer crisis intervention
independent living centers	advocate for individuals or groups
meal delivery programs	collect clothing
employment services	organize entertainment
nursing homes	do job development

court programs
shelters
children's advocacy groups
community centers
hotlines
halfway houses
sheltered workshops
runaway programs
women's centers

provide information / referrals
drive
offer clerical assistance
teach socialization skills
do friendly visiting
telephone reassurance
be a big brother / sister
assist recreational therapy
deliver food
play games
lead discussion groups

3) EDUCATION

Types of Programs:
public schools
adult education classes
programs for foreign born
community centers
senior citizen centers
youth programs
vocational programs
after school programs
special schools
literacy programs
h.s. equivalency programs
nursing homes
rehabilitation hospitals
education / training committees
health / safety programs
programs for the retarded

Responsibilities:
tutor in any subject
teach adults to read
act as a role model
converse in English with foreign
    born
set up courses
do research
teach a trade
teach first aid / water safety
provide homework help
assist teachers in schools
share a hobby or skill
teach a sport or game
train volunteers
lead discussion groups
advocate
serve on a committee
do public speaking

4) CULTURAL ACTIVITIES

Types of Programs:
museums
community theatre
historic houses
public TV
schools
nursing homes
community centers
arts and crafts programs
art galleries
street theatres
zoos

Responsibilities:
serve as a docent
build exhibits
design public relations programs
type
translate material and ideas
provide information
train volunteers
provide clerical assistance
do research
serve on boards / committees
work in a gift shop

public radio
hospitals
botanical gardens
dance companies
libraries

greet visitors
serve as a host / hostess
be a box office clerk
teach arts and crafts
help care for animals
teach photography
garden
organize entertainment
work backstage

5) RECREATION

Types of Programs:
senior citizen centers
nursing homes
rehabilitation programs
museums
criminal justice programs
community centers
correctional facilities
settlement houses
hospitals
day care centers
parks
zoos
youth centers
schools
youth organizations
after school programs

Responsibilities:
assist occupational therapists
conduct yoga classes
teach music
assist with drama classes
teach plant care
type
run photography workshops
play board games
coach a team
be a tour guide
assist in arts and crafts
run a sports program
be a performer
help with animal care
be a swimming instructor
be a big brother / sister
lead discussion groups
teach dance
teach a sport
lead activity groups

6) PUBLIC INTEREST

Types of Programs:
community agencies
school boards
business assistance programs
tenant associations
women's issues
animal welfare
housing
self-help
criminal justice agencies
correction
service to inmates

Responsibilities:
plan
write
provide information / referrals
advocate
serve as court liaison
locate and care for animals
give paralegal assistance
survey community needs
advise small businesses
coordinate projects / programs
speak on issues

community boards
governmental agencies
neighborhood organizations
special interest groups
environment
consumerism
social action
probation
crime prevention

research
monitor legislative process
train
counsel
provide financial counseling
perform clerical tasks
work in public relations
lobby for legislation
canvass and petition[23]

---

[23] "Volunteer...Where the Action Is!", Volunteer Service Bureau (White Plains, NY, 1984).

PERSONAL INVESTMENTS.

Don't let the title fool you. Although this chapter is called Personal Investments it doesn't deal with subjects like how to buy a condo, invest in savings bonds, play the stock market. You'll have to phone E. F. Hutton for that.

What this chapter focuses on is developing certain skills and characteristics that are important for personal growth, regardless of what you choose to do. Learning to be more assertive is an example of the kind of trait that can enhance your life whether you work, go back to school or travel. Elevating self-image is another. So is maintaining a positive outlook. In fact, just browse through the "how-to" section of any bookstore and you'll find hundreds of ways you can better equip yourself for the life you select after college. From decision-making skills to leadership abilities, communication arts to self-motivation, you'll discover a long list of personal investments, that will help you reach your potential, no matter which direction you head in.

Whether your initial reason for concentrating on a personal investment is for business gains, pleasure or spiritual growth — you'll find the rewards of fine-tuning certain characteristics are endless! Learning to reduce stress, for instance, can decrease everyday tension, alleviate mental disorders, even reduce the incidence of heart disease. Developing social skills can open new doors in the workplace, home and leisure settings. Learning to direct anger effectively can eliminate anxiety, depression and actually improve relationships. The list goes on. After taking a course on successful negotiation, I not only convinced my roommate to clean our apartment, I persuaded my boss to give me a raise. And if you knew my boss, Mr. Tightwad, you'd realize just how powerful are the skills I learned.

Now more than ever, a vast number of resources are available that provide instruction. A rising number of community groups, schools and colleges offer courses on particular personal-development skills. Practically every general interest magazine has an article or two on how to be more confident, perfect analytical skills, become more motivated. A wide range of cassettes, books, TV shows, even corporate programs are available to make challenges, like giving a speech, much easier.

Of course the rate at which you cultivate something like leadership skills depends upon the amount of time and energy you put into it. Certainly an hour-long lecture won't change you as drastically as a lifetime of cumulative effort. But even one hour devoted to a personal investment can make important differences.

Wait until you bump into someone you haven't seen since high school. You'll easily be able to distinguish whether the person is someone who works hard to improve him or herself or whether he or she sits back and does nothing. Speech, mannerisms, goals and activities are easy indicators.

Every time I speak to Andrea she's taking another seminar on effective speech. In fact, she's become so proficient in speaking before groups that she's started a business doing just that. Companies, friends, skilled professionals are now hiring her to give presentations they feel incapable of tackling. Andrea is gaining exposure, contacts and valuable experience all because she worked on her communications skills.

Andrea is a good example of how a person can improve specific skills to enhance life personally, professionally and socially. Not everyone will want to turn a personal investment into a business like Andrea did. But practically all facets of your life will progress when you take the time to develop yourself. Let's look at a few personal investments and see how they can influence your life.

EFFECTIVE COMMUNICATION

When I was a freshman in college we had the heating system in our house changed from electric to gas. My parents got a good price on the conversion but it had to be done in November. Nobody minded the wait, until we realized we'd have to do without heat until the final hook-up was made.

It was just our luck the cold weather came early that year. So the family walked around with heaps of clothing on. What made matters worse was the fact that the plumber kept miscalculating his completion date.

Every day each of us would call from work, school, wherever, hoping to hear "The heat is on." Instead, an annoyed, rather desperate voice said, "Maybe tomorrow." (You may have noticed that my family isn't the pioneer-type.)

It was an exceptionally cold day mid-month and I sat at my part-ime job imagining how nice it would be not to wear a coat to bed or gloves to dinner. (You think it's easy eating artichokes with mittens on?) My thoughts of saying, "Good morning," without vapor billowing from my lips were interrupted by a call from home.

It was my sister. "Do me a favor," she pleaded. "Don't call today to see if the heat is on. You'll upset everyone. The plumber was here and he just blew apart."

"Is he dead?" I asked frantically imagining pieces of him scattered all over the basement.

"No," she said. "He burned out a piece of the system."

It's easy to misinterpret people. Speech patterns, voice inflections and a wide variety of mannerisms, accents, idioms, can make a simple statement like "How nice" anything from a compliment to a sarcastic put-down. That's why it's so important for people to be sure they are communicating properly as well as being interpreted correctly.

You can probably think of countless dilemmas that have occurred just because someone misinterpreted what you said. Or what you said wasn't expressed clearly. There are easily many misconstrued written communications too.

It happens constantly in business. For some reason when many people sit down to write a business letter, they suddenly feel compelled to create a literary masterpiece. Instead of writing a clear, succinct dispatch, people tend to mull over their letter loading it with high-falutin wordage. It's unnecessary. Thinking through the purpose of the message, jotting down key points to highlight, and writing your message in easy language will help to eliminate confusion.

Effective written and oral communication can make a difference in your life. Not only can it help you speak and write more succinctly, it will help you interpret what others say and write too.

Strictly Speaking: Will America Be The Death Of English? by Edwin Newman illustrates the point further. You might want to pick up a copy as a starting point to more effective communications.

SELF-MOTIVATION

For some people, nothing is harder than getting motivated. I have a very good friend who started his own design business. Most people who use his services do so because the name of the firm indicates he'll design a room, deck or office with new and unique style. But that's only one of the reasons the business is named Creative Environment. The other is that he actually created an atmosphere for himself — one where he can get up and go to work when he feels motivated.

Not all of us will be able to develop a business around the talents and lifestyle my friend leads. Most will work within the confines society dictates.

If you're a person who has trouble getting motivated perhaps you should look into ways you can develop that part of your personality. Even though it seems paradoxical learning to be self-motivated takes motivation itself. There are ways to improve.

Many people use a method called affirmations to get them going. An affirmation is a positive statement they compose that describes specifically what they want to be, what they want to have and how they want to direct their lives. By writing the affirmation, saying it over again and picturing it mentally, many boast positive results. If you put energy into it, positive thinking really does have power.

Some attack hard, seemingly endless projects by taking small pokes at them. By accomplishing the easier, less burdensome portions of a job, the total project doesn't appear as overwhelming.

Rewarding yourself in various stages helps too. I remember exam week. There was no one who ate more than me. I'd study a chapter, have a sandwich. Memorize a theorem, eat a box cookies. Reread my notes, go for pizza.

Of course, there are many less fattening ways to develop self-motivation. Psychologists claim that anger and competitive feelings can be turned into motivation. So can frustration, ideas of inadequacy and peer pressure.

If you have a tough time becoming a self-starter, why not read some books, articles, listen to tapes or take a course? A lot of resources are available. After all, developing self-motivation is nothing new. Even Plato left us with these encouraging words: "Take charge of your life, you can do what you will with it."

LISTENING

While eating lunch alone recently, at a little joint in town, I overheard this conversation.

"I don't think I can afford school next semester. My usual summer job was filled by someone else, my parents can't swing the payments, and I don't think I can take out a big enough loan. I'm so depressed. If I stop school now I'll probably never finish. What am I going to do, Maryann? Do you have any ideas?"

To which Maryann replied, "Did I tell you I made the dean's list?"

We all know lousy listeners. Maybe they're not as bad as Maryann, yet we all know people who interrupt, complete our sentences, ask questions we've already answered and, like Maryann, change the subject midway through our idea. It's very frustrating!

Listening is a more demanding process than hearing. In this example, I'm sure Maryann could hear her friend speaking. The question is, was Maryann concentrating on the words that were being spoken? Was she translating her friend's words, gestures, facial expressions into concrete messages? My guess is no.

Listening is an important skill to learn and one that requires practice. Especially since it involves just about everything we do — from a friend's account of last night's party to a professor's view of recent history. From a doctor's orders to employee's requests, father's suggestions to brother's plea for advice — listening is an integral part of life for all those lucky enough to be able to hear.

So why are too many people poor listeners? For starters, effective listening is not something taught or practiced as stringently as it should. For years we've all been lectured on written and oral communications. How many of us have ever been taught auditory communication?

In addition, personality differences can cause poor listening habits. Selfish people are often weak at this. Some are so anxious to get their point across that, while you're speaking, they're actually thinking of the next thing to say. Maryann is probably guilty of this.

Shyness can affect listening. Often introverted people look like they're paying attention while their minds are occupied with fears of having to speak. Severe prejudices can also affect listening skills. People often hold such strong opinions that, as soon as a challenging statement is made, they stop concentrating.

Since each of us can use help developing listening habits, here are a few tips:

• Resist distractions. A girl who worked at the campus deli applied her make-up in two big circles around her eyes. It was so hideous that every time she asked, "What would you like?" I'd have to ask her what she said. I couldn't keep my eyes off her bizarre make-up.

• Observe body language such as hand gestures and facial expressions, in relation to what a person's saying. Listening to a speaker involves more than just hearing words.

• If you don't understand something, ask. It's all part of the communication process. Besides it shows you're paying attention.

• Be patient when listening. Let ideas seep in rather than racing to respond.

• Encourage a speaker with positive feedback. An appropriate nod or smile not only shows you're interested, it encourages the speaker to continue.

• Like communication arts and self-motivation, listening is a worthwhile skill to develop and constantly work on.

Certainly there is a long list of others you may choose to enhance. Whether you devote one hour a year or eight hours a day, improving personal investments can help you reach your potential in the workplace, home and social arenas.

CLOSING

Aim for a star! Never be satisfied
With a life that is less than the best,
Failure lies only in not having tried —
In keeping the soul suppressed.
Aim for a star! Look up and away
Make each tommorow a better today.
And don't be afraid to dream.
Aim for a star!
And keep your sights high.
With a heart full of faith within,
Your feet on the ground, and
Your eyes on the sky!
Some day you are bound to win.

— Helen L. Marshall

I hope that *Life After College* will help you reach the star you're aiming for. With a solid goal chart established, a well-thought-out set of priorities, a grasp on how to make sound decisions, and instructions on how to attain the path you've chosen, you are better equipped to attain all the accomplishments you desire.

And no matter what path you've chosen, if life throws some obstacles in your way, I hope also that you'll manipulate them in a way the lead character did in the short story "The Verger." An illiterate man was the verger in a small local church. He was responsible for sacred vessels, vestments, ringing bells, etc., until an ordinance was passed by higher officials demanding that all vergers be able to read and write. The main character was devastated and, needless to say, out of a job. So he opened a small smoke shop in town. To his surprise it flourished. He opened another with the same success, and he kept parlaying his business into bigger and more profitable establishments. One day the lead character's accountant sat figuring his net worth. Astounded by his great wealth, the accountant exclaimed, "It's amazing with all your money, repect and business savvy, you can't read or write. Can you imagine what you'd be today if you could?"

And the main character simply said, "Yes, I'd be a verger."

Good luck with your life after college!

APPENDICES.

The following chart lists some of the most popular master's and doctoral programs available:[24]

English Language & Literature	History
Mathematics	Chemistry
Biology	Physics
Psychology	Music
Economics	Political Science
Sociology	Speech
French Language	Philosophy
Art	Hispanic Language & Literature
Drama	Geology
German Language & Literature	Microbiology
Anthropology	Speech Disorders & Audiology
Biochemistry	Zoology
Geography	Speech Pathology & Audiology
Social Science	Government
Physiology	Pharmacology
Fine & Applied Arts	Anatomy
Bacteriology	Statistics
Classics	Art History
Comparative Literature	Linguistics
Russian & Slavic Language & Literature	Modern Language
	Entomology
Child Development & Family Relations	Am. Civilization
	Metallurgy

---

[24] Lewis B. Mayhew, *Graduate & Professional Education* (New York: McGraw Hill Book Co., 1970), pp. 34–38.

Journalism
Genetics
Classical Language & Literature
Italian Language & Literature
Biophysics
Communications
Fisheries & Wildlife
Interdivisional & Area Studies
Industrial Relations
Public & International Affairs
Far Eastern Language &
    Literature
Meteorology
Oceanography
Labor Management Relations
Indian & Far Eastern Language
    & Literature
Medieval Studies
Limnology
History of Mathematics
Classical Civilization
Folklore
Chinese Art & Archeology

Musicology
International Relations
Child Psychology
Public Health
Astronomy
Social Psychology
Marine Biology
Geochemistry
Human Development
Mineralogy
Portuguese Language &
    Literature
Biostatistics
Near Eastern Language &
    Literature
History of Science
Mass Communications
Oriental Studies
Semitic & Egyptian Language
    & Literature
Social Thought
Biopsychology
Egyptology

Doctoral Programs Offered:

Chemistry
Psychology
History
English Language & Literature
Physiology
Pharmacology
Sociology
Philosophy
Anatomy
Bacteriology
Anthropology
German Language & Literature
Biophysics
Entomology
Metallurgy
Government
Linguistics
Astronomy
Fisheries & Wildlife
Speech Disorders & Audiology
Russian & Slavic Language & Lit.

Physics
Mathematics
Biochemistry
Economics
Biology
Political Science
Geology
Botany
Zoology
Hispanic Language & Literature
French Language & Literature
Genetics
Statistics
Comparative Lit.
Geography
Music
Speech Pathology & Audiology
Speech
Art History
Drama & Theater
Geochemistry

Musicology
Italian Language & Literature
Marine Biology
International Relations
Interdivisional & Area Studies
Meteorology
Far Eastern Language &
  Literature
Near Eastern Language &
  Literature
Mass Communications
Public & International Affairs
Communications
Child Development & Family
  Relations
Labor Management Relations
Journalism
Medieval Studies
Social Science
Portuguese Language &
  Literature
Fine & Applied Arts
History of Mathematics

Social Psychology
Classics
Child Psychology
Public Health
Am. Civilization
Classical Language & Literature
Oceanography
Mineralogy
Biostatistics
Limnology
History of Science
Modern Language
Classical Civilization
Indian & Far Eastern Language
  & Literature
Human Development
Industrial Relations
Semitic & Egyptian Lang. & Lit.
Social Thought
Folklore
Egyptology
Biopsychology
Oriental Studies

1) Directory of Graduate Programs 1985/86
Four separate volumes are available—including biology and allied field; humanities; physical sciences, mathematics; and social sciences and education.

Look for it in the college library, public library or by writing:

Graduate Record Examinations
Educational Testing Services
CN 4681
Trenton, NJ 08650-4681

2) Peterson's Annual Guide to Graduate Study
Look for this in the college and public libraries.

3) And for those who go beyond graduate school...
An Assessment of Research Doctorate Programs in U.S.
published by the National Academy of Sciences

This book reviews 2,700 PhD programs in 32 disciplines!

GRADUATE SCHOOL LOANS

The following are a number of special loans offered for graduate study. For additional information on each, like your rights as a borrower, deferment, repayment, etc. write:

> Department of Health Education & Welfare
> Bureau of Student Financial Assistance
> Washington, DC 20202

1) National Direct Student Loans

- These are low interest loans (interest rate about 5%) based on: your need; the other financial aid you're receiving and the amount of funds available at the school you'll be attending.

- The amount you borrowed for undergraduate study is also taken into consideration, if applicable.

- Repayment usually begins six months after graduation and you usually have up to 10 years to complete.

- Contact the financial aid administrator at your school for an application and deadline information.

2) Guaranteed Student Loans

- Credit unions, banks, savings and loan associations provide low interest loans to students who need help paying tuition.

- You can borrow up to $5,000 yearly (in some states it's lower) and as much as $25,000 in total (including undergraduate loans).

- Can get Guaranteed Student Loan application from school, state or lending institution.

- Inquire as soon as you're accepted at a school.

3) Plus Loans

- Like the Guaranteed Student Loans, these are made by banks, credit unions, savings and loan associations to provide additional funds for educational expenses.

- You may borrow up to $3,000 a year and as much as $15,000 in total in addition to any Guaranteed Student Loans you may have.

- Apply the same way you would for Guaranteed Student Loans.

Since funding and its particulars change from year to year, it's better to write the Department of Health, Education & Welfare for details on assistance. You may also want to pick up a copy of the following:

> *How To Beat The High Cost of Learning*
> By Leo L. Kornfield, Connie McClung Siegel and
> William Laird Siegel
> Published by Rawson, Wade Publishers, Inc., NY 1981

A number of special loans are available for medical students. Check into the Health Education Assistance Loan (HEAL), as well as the National Service Corps Scholarship and the Health Professions Student Loan. Write: U.S. Department of Health & Human Services. In addition, women can write: American Medical Women's Associations Medical Education Loan Program, Loan Department, 465 Grand Street, NY, NY 10002 or call (212) 533-5104.

Some student aid programs specifically help members of minority groups. For information write the Consusmer Information Center for the guide on Higher Education Opportunities for Minorities and Women, Annotated Selections, send $5.50 to Dept. 185P, Pueblo, CO 81009.

To Be Eligible For Financial Aid You Must Meet These Requirements:

1) Show financial need.
2) Be a US citizen or eligible non-citizen (ex. US permanent resident who has a I-151 or F-551).
3) Be enrolled at least ½ time as a regular student in an eligible program at one of more than 7,000 colleges, universities, technical schools, hospital schools, that take part in Department of Education's Financial Aid Programs.
4) Meet the standard of academic progress determined by the school you want to attend.
5) Are not in default of a National Direct Student Loan, Guaranteed Student Loan or PLUS loan at the school you attend.
6) Don't owe a refund on a Pell Grant or Supplemental Educational Opportunity Grant at the school you attend.
7) Are registered with selective service if you're required to do so.
8) And only use the money for educational purposes.

*Information is taken from the Student Guide issued by the Department of Health, Education and Welfare.

APPENDIX B
ADDITIONAL SOURCES
FOR TRAVEL INFORMATION

Travel information for taking a cruise on a freighter or cargo-carrying vessel can be obtained by writing:

Ford's Freighter Travel Guide
PO Box 505
Woodland Hills, CA 91365

Sources for additional travel information:

1) *Consumer's Guide to Package Travel Around the World*
   by Frederick Pratson
   published by Globe Pequot Press, CT

   Hot air ballooning in France, budget stays in the Caribbean, treks through Nepal and more. A listing of over 200 tour operators and what they offer.

2) *Global Employment Guide*
   by James N. Powell
   published by Farnsworth Publishing Co., NY

   Worldwide opportunities for profitable year-round or seasonal work.

3) Details on national parks and monuments can be obtained from:
   The National Park Service
   U.S. Dept. of Interior
   Washington, D.C. 20240

4) For travel agencies and tour operators who cater to the handicapped write:
   Society for the Advancement of Travel for the Handicapped
   26 Court St.
   Brooklyn, NY 11242
   (718) 858-5483

   Travel/Ability
   by Lois Remy
   published by Macmillan Publishing Co., NY

5) Here's how to get a listing of 2,700 items and the 90 countries and 40 territories that allow duty-free exports, write:
   Department of Treasury
   U.S. Customs Service
   1301 Constitution Ave., NW
   Washington, D.C. 20229

6) *Finding the Best Place to Live in America*
   by Dr. Thomas F. Bowman, Dr. George A. Guiliani &
   Dr. M. Ronald Minge
   published by Warner Books, NY

7) For an unbiased look at some cultural customs of other countries
   send $0.35 and a self-addressed stamped envelope (SASE) to:
   "Culturgrams"
   Brigham Young University Center for International & Area Studies
   Box 61-X FOB
   Provo, UT 84606 (801) 378-6528

8) How about some background notes on countries throughout the
   world? Write:
   Superintendents of Documents
   U.S. Government Printing Office
   Washington, D.C. 20402 (202) 783-3238

9) Take a look at adverse political, health and weather conditions, call:
   State Dept. Citizen's Emergency Center
   (202) 632-5225

10) Rights as an airline passenger? Write:
    Consumers Affairs
    International Airline Passenger Association
    4301 West Side Drive
    Dallas, TX 75209
    (214) 520-1070

11) Here's how to bring merchandise back home:
    U.S. Customs Service
    World Trade Center
    New York, NY 10048
    (212) 466-5550

APPENDIX C
ASSESSING YOUR INTERESTS AND SKILLS

1) Re-read the chapter on goal-setting and decision-making, as well as other books and articles on the subject.

2) Visit your college or university career-placement center or arrange to visit one in your area. Ask if they offer such vocational tests as *Discover* and *ETS-SIGI*, that is if you haven't already taken one. Try to speak to an advisor. Many have a battery of questions and discovery methods they've developed over the years and use successfully. Dr. Jennifer B. Kahnweiler, Director of Career Development at the University of Cincinnati, says, "A growing trend on campuses throughout the country is to have a strong alumni placement program. In addition, most colleges and universities welcome graduates back for workshops and seminars. In fact, many alumni tell me they're sorry they didn't take advantage of these services as undergraduates."

3) Compose an autobiographical sketch. Then analyze it for trends, strengths, interests and skills. This is beneficial, since it can be used as a guide to writing a good résumé.

4) Consider one of the employment counselors who'll assist you, for a fee ranging from $25 to $100 an hour. They're listed in the Yellow Pages of the phone directory. However, with all the good free help available, I don't recommend paying a private counselor for aid, unless he or she comes very highly recommended.

If you do go to a private counselor, be sure to ask him for a list of references you can check. Ask if he is certified, what his track record has been, and what specific services he offers. And most importantly, don't sign anything unless you understand it thoroughly.

5) You might also want to try the local branch of the U.S. Employment Agency. They offer a job service where diagnostic tests are given free-of-charge. As a matter of fact, the agency administers an evaluation very similar to those given by private counselors. A word of caution though — while the evaluation is very helpful, these U.S. job service bureaus tend to handle job-seekers looking for lower-level jobs.

Although some of these methods are more highly recommended than others, each can help you learn more about your skills, traits and desires.

APPENDIX D
INFORMATION ABOUT JOBS

1) *Dictionary of Occupational Titles*
   Published by the U.S. Employment Service, Washington, D.C.

This book categorizes occupations by field, then gives a brief description of each job and its function within that field.

2) *The National Directory — An Occupational Information Handbook*
   By Barry and Linda Gale
   Published By Arco Publishers, Inc., NY

A directory of over 2,000 references to free printed material and information available on entrance and training requirements, specific duties involved, earnings, growth possibilities and personal satisfactions.

3) *Encyclopedia of Careers and Vocational Guidance*
   Editor-in-Chief: William E. Hopke
   Published by J. G. Ferguson Publishing Co., Chicago

Defines and explains over 650 occupations. Volume I offers ideas, guidance and the general flavor of important areas of work. Volume II gives specific information on careers: nature of work, history, special and educational requirements, methods of entry, advancement, employment outlook, conditions of work, social and psychological factors and sources of additional information.

APPENDIX E
INFORMATION INTERVIEWING

Information interviewing begins with gathering a list of people who'll be able to offer sound advice. There are a number of ways to gather contacts:

People you know. Any family members, friends, members of a mutual community organization, church, synagogue, health club who work in a field, company or hold positions that interest you, should be consulted.

Alumni listings. Most colleges and universities have a career placement and development department that offers a listing of alumni by field. These are perfect candidates to get in touch with since you already have something in common, namely your alma mater.

Directories. The list of directories goes on and on. Here are some that will certainly help you reach key people. In fact, you'll be advised to refer to this list in the next section since they are also great volumes for company information:

1) *Encyclopedia of Associations*
   Editor — Margaret Fisk
   Published By Gale Research Co., Detroit

This guide to over 18,000 national and international organizations is terrific for finding people in your area of interest. From agriculture to religious organizations, cultural to health and medical, readers can cull contacts, addresses and phone numbers to start them on their search.

2) *Directory of Corporate Affiliations*
   published by National Register Publishing Co., Inc., Skokie

A volume that presents an in-depth view of major U.S. corporations, their divisions, affiliates, subsidiaries. Again company names, addresses and phone numbers will get you started.

3) *The 100 Best Companies To Work For In America*
   By Robert Levering, Milton Moskowitz, Michael Katz
   Published by Addison–Wesley Publishing Co., Reading

In addition to it being a great source on specific companies, benefits, job security, ambience and pay rates, it will put you in touch with influentials.

4) *Standard & Poor's Corporate Records*
   published by Standard & Poor's Corp., New York
Again this is a vital source for company employee information.

5) *The Macmillan Job Guide to American Corporations*
   Edited By Ernest A. Mackay
   Published by Macmillan Co., New York

Profiles of the top 260 U.S. corporations are provided as well as, facts on branch offices, requirements, benefits, annual sales, etc.

Most of these sources can be found in your library along with other major references. Although they don't necessarily list the people you'll want to interview, they do supply the address and phone number of each company. By calling and asking the receptionist for the name of the department head or person who fills a position of interest, you're on your way to writing a letter of inquiry. In addition, these sources will also furnish background on companies you'll be calling. This information will be imperative when finally going on your information interview, as well as your job interview. Having concrete facts shows you're truly interested, well-informed and a real go-getter. Here are some other ways to find people to interview:

Local Sources. Your local chamber of commerce and telephone directory will supply you with names and addresses of businesses in your area. These are especially good sources for graduates interested in smaller companies that wouldn't be listed in the directories mentioned above.

Periodicals. Annual reports are a good source of data and so are journals, newspapers, magazines. For current articles on specific fields and companies, look in the *Business Periodicals Index* at the library. Names of key people may be lifted and contacted from these.

Once you've compiled a list of contacts you're ready to set up appointments. Although you may be timid at first, keep in mind that information interviewing is a common practice. Besides, people love to give advice and talk about themselves, so they'll be glad to help.

The most professional way to ask for an appointment is to write a brief introductory letter to your contact. (Of course, a relative or friend you can probably just call, depending on your relationship.) Explain your objective — that you would like to discuss trends, goals, issues of a particular field, position, company. The more specific you are the better your results will be. You might want to write how you got his or her name, especially if you were referred by a friend or relative or read about him or her recently. Close with a statement that you'll be calling soon to arrange an appointment. The sample letter on page 138 may be of further assistance.

It's a smart practice to keep a diary of everyone you contacted, and the day, date and time, so that duplicate letters won't be sent, phone calls will be timely and appointments kept.

When you phone to arrange a meeting introduce yourself, state the nature of your call and check to see that the letter was received. If this is done with the secretary because the contact is busy, then ask, "When is the best time to call back?" Be pleasant, polite and don't be insulted if the person doesn't remember you right away.

Matthew Truden
4362 Lindell Blvd.
St. Louis, MO 63108
September 20, 1987

Ms. Catherine Knudsen
Druson & Gray Marketing Association
5455 Harlan Court
St. Louis, MO 63112

Dear Ms. Knudsen:

As a driver for the Garden Shed Florists in St. Louis, I've often made deliveries to Druson & Gray Marketing Association and most often to you. I was always very intrigued by your firm as well as impressed by the awards displayed in the lobby.

In December I graduated from the University of Texas at El Paso, with a business degree in marketing. I am gathering some information on direct mail and would like very much to discuss trends that have changed customer response to the direct mail industry.

I will call you next week to arrange an appointment.

Sincerely,

Matthew Truden

Usually the best time to information interview is right after office hours so that you don't interfere with work schedules nor will you feel compelled to pick up a lunch tab you really can't afford.

Terrific, you've got an appointment! Now what? Do as much business research about the specific interviewee as possible. That includes the company, field and position he has. Write a list of specific questions you'd like to ask. (The section on decision-making deals with consulting an expert. It might be a good refresher.) And remember to be polite, enthusiastic and professional. Just because this isn't a job interview doesn't mean you should cut corners. In fact, read the section on job interviews to be sure you dress and handle yourself properly.

The meeting should last 30–45 minutes unless the interviewee doesn't mind giving more time. Be assertive, confident, ask meaningful questions, such as the person's thoughts, opinions, ideas and reactions to any relative issues. Discuss your objectives to date. And never ask for a job. This is an information interview not a job interview. (Although it has been reported that some do get lucky and are offered a position.) Jot down notes, ask about other books, literature you can read and other contacts you can write. Most importantly, always thank the person for his/her time and follow up with a brief note of gratitude.

Hopefully information interviewing will bring you closer to focusing on a specific field, company and position you'll enjoy. Of course, just because you've decided to become a systems analyst for IBM doesn't mean you'll get the job, but you'll have a much better chance by following the tips in this section as well as the next.

APPENDIX F
CALLING FOR AN INTERVIEW

First call the company and ask to speak to the appropriate department head. Remember to find out his/her name first, so that you can address the person professionally.

a) introduce yourself — include your first and last names.

b) explain the purpose of the call — state the position you desire by being specific and brief.

c) discuss the skills you can offer — any relative experience, activities, volunteer work. (Keep it short.)

d) then ask for an interview — this may sound pushy but "three out of ten jobs do not exist until the right person appears and a job is created for that person."[25] If you are able to set up an appointment, determine a definite date and time to meet.

Be polite, professional and enthusiastic. Rehearse your call by referring to notes. But don't read them, otherwise you might sound very stilted and mechanical. Some people practice by tape recording a mock call. Often when they play it back they realize they don't sound as smooth, assertive, etc. as they'd like. Others practice by calling the least favorite company they'd like to work for first.

Some companies insist that you speak to the personnel department before you contact the department you're interested in working for. If you can avoid it, do so. It's better to get directly to your potential employer.

You may also have to deal with a very inquisitive secretary. If you're given the third degree, be creative and think of a way to bypass severe inquisition. Why not say you're returning Mr./Ms. ————'s call? Or that you're calling about brokerage trends, market values, etc.?

And don't be surprised if some department heads are upset by your call. If an irate manager tries to intimidate you, think of it as an exercise in perseverance. Politely end the conversation then try the next company on your list.

If you had an information interview with someone who can help, give him/her a call. Re-introduce yourself, remind the person who you are and follow steps b–d. If no position is available, perhaps she knows another available position in the industry.

Ask the person you're speaking with if sending a résumé will help. There are occasions when an employer is aware that a position will open up soon. When you do mail your résumé, be sure to write about the discussion you had in your cover letter. Anything that will separate you favorably from the competition is worth the extra effort.

---

[25] Shirley Sloan Fader, *loc. cit.*

So whom do you call? You already know the field and position you're interested in seeking. The next step is to explore companies you'd like to work for. Appendix E lists some references that might lead you to prospective employers. In addition to these directories, there are a number of other valuable sources for reference. Let's take a look:

— large national and international firms can be found in business to business directories such as the *Thomas Register of American Manufacturers* and *Everybody's Business An Almanac / The Irreverent Guide to Corporate America*. These are only two of many volumes that can be found on companies in most libraries. Also you can consult trade journals and major magazines.

— information on local businesses, that are not as world renowned as those published in library references, can be found by calling the Chamber of Commerce, by looking through the Yellow Pages and White Pages of the phone book and by reading local newspapers, magazines and trade publications.

At one point in my career I decided to try something I never had before. While leafing through a local marketing circular, I noticed an article on an advertising president who was relocating his company from Manhattan to the surburbs. So I wrote him a letter telling him how thrilled I was that more agencies were moving into my area. Naturally I referred to the publication in which the article appeared, discussed a few of the accounts he represented and skills I had to offer. It took a one page cover letter, a résumé, and a stamp to get myself an interview.

APPENDIX G
ANSWERING NEWSPAPER ADS

Job leads publicized in trade journals and newspapers, may be found under a variety of different headings. For example a copywriting position may be placed under advertising; public relations; or writing. Be thorough and check all relevant headings.

—look for ads in different sections of a publication. At times a position may be placed in the regular classified section, at others, in a section that relates to the field: business section, health & medicine, etc.

— even though Wednesday and Sunday are the "big" days for newspaper classifieds, it's a good idea to follow ads everyday. A jump on the competition can mean a chance for an interview.

— answer ads immediately. It will give you a headstart on competition.

— think twice about answering an ad that doesn't identify the employer. These are usually "market studies" or an employment agency's "file boosters."

— tailor your cover letter to each ad. If a company is seeking an administrative assistant for its market research division, point out your telemarketing experience.

— ads that ask for salary requirements can be handled in two ways. The first would be to state that salary is negotiable. The second would be to give a ballpark figure based on the marketplace. This can be determined by calling a friend / relative in the field who knows, looking at the salary ranges of similar jobs listed in the classifieds, and by consulting salary ranges through the U.S. Employment Agency or through references at the library.

A classified ad is a breed unto itself. It's got its own advantages, disadvantages, requirements and competitive edges. Classified ads have even got their own language. This chart should help you translate an employer's requests:

Want-Ad Lingo

Example	Explanation
15M	$15,000 is the salary offered
	M = 1000 in Roman numerials
25K	since K = kilo which is Greek for 1000, 25K means $25,000 is offered annually for the job
exp. reqd.	experience required
$25k +	means salary negotiation starts at $25,000 and will go higher based on experience
to 23K	salary offer is up to $23,000 a year
F / pd	fee paid — when you go to the agency that is advertising the job, the fee will be paid by the employer who is seeking help

No fee	same as above
Send résumé which must include salary requirements	can send salary range based on marketplace or can say salary is negotiable. This should be written in the cover letter.
Sal open	salary is negotiable within reason. The salary range is usually in keeping with the market.
$20K base + comm.	the yearly salary will be $20,000 plus a commission on the % of the business you generate.
salary competitive	the yearly salary is in keeping with what competitive companies pay comparable positions
teachers (2)	there are two positions available
refs	references wanted, include in cover letter
F68777 News 00000	if you send your résumé to a box number, don't count on a response. Often employment agencies and executive search firms generate applicants this way.
no calls	if they took the time to include this in the ad, then don't call.
pfd	preferred
pt	part time
ft	full time
EOE	equal opportunity employer
appt	appointment
ofc	office
bkgd nec	background necessary

APPENDIX H
PERSONNEL AGENCIES

Don't pay a fee! Although some people believe the more you pay for something the better it is, the theory isn't necessarily true with this type of agency. First of all, no matter how much you pay someone, they're never going to be as interested in your needs and desires as you are. (Unless that person is your mother.) As enticing as some agencies may sound, professionals have been known to make empty promises for jobs that are far beyond any recent graduate's league. However, if you'd like to spend some money on that first career-type job, why not take a seminar on job-hunting techniques? One of the most highly acclaimed is given by Richard Nelson Bolles, author of the best selling title, *What Color Is Your Parachute?* Write the National Career Development Project, PO Box 379, Walnut Creek, CA 94597.

Never sign a contract unless you're absolutely sure what you're signing! What may seem like a good deal now, may become a sour one. Some agencies ask for exclusive rights or other such privileges you may object to later on. If you're feeling pressured to sign an agreement, take the form home, re-read it and ask someone with more experience for advice. You can even call the Better Business Bureau in your area, to investigate if the agency has had any complaints filed against them. It's easy to check and it can spare you a lot of headaches.

Use private personnel agencies as one source among many! Painting a grim picture of personnel agencies isn't totally justified. After all, if they didn't get job-seekers work, they wouldn't be in business. Although they might not have lived up to your friend's expectations, now that you've read this section you'll be better prepared and less likely to rely on one solely.

Look for counselors that are certified! A certified personnel consultant (CPC) usually guarantees you're dealing with someone with know-how. In order to be certified a counselor must have worked in the field at least two years and must have passed an exam covering laws affecting employment, general business practice and situational problems. Unfortunately, CPCs comprise a small percentage of the consultant population.

Ask Questions! How long has a consultant been in the field? What services does the agency offer? How much time will they spend with you? Is a fee involved? How much? What about a contract?

APPENDIX I
WRITING A RESUME

The following tips refer to the sample résumé on page 146:

Identity. You'll notice the sample first lists the job-seeker's name, address, city, state, zip, area code and home phone number. An applicant who can be reached at a different number during the day, or has a reliable friend or relative who can relay a message, should be sure to mention it in the cover letter. Two unanswered calls may be all an employer needs to never try again.

Personal. There's a lot of controversy over whether or not personal data should appear on a résumé. This would include such details as height, weight, marital status, age and health condition. First of all, facts like this can cause discrimination. Secondly, they have little relevance to whether you are capable of handling a specific job. Of course, there are a few occupations where personal characteristics are imperative. But not many. So the decision to include them is yours. Personal information on a chronological résumé most often appears in one of two places:

alongside of identity:

Peggy Runleck   24 years old
18 Farrow Rd.   single
Washington, DC 20044   5'6", 120 lbs.
(202) 661-2181   health: excellent

or underneath identity:

Peter MacCormack
1616 Delaware Turnpike
Arlington, VA 22212
(703) 823-2184
Personal: 25 years old, single, 6'2", 175 lbs., good health

Career Objective. This is another detail you can decide whether or not to include on your résumé. Many decide they'd rather include it in their cover letter, others do both. The sample résumé shows a career objective. Potential employers often encourage a candidate to include one, since knowing what you want will help them decide if and where they'll place you. Of course, if you're sending a résumé in response to an advertisement, it will be clear for an employer to see what your objective is. Just be sure to refer to the ad and position you're applying for in the cover letter.

Education. When a job applicant has very little career-related experience, often he or she will place college education on his résumé before work experience. Under education the applicant should include

Claire Stratton
7 Lingo Lane
Newark, NJ 07102
(210) 869-6162

<u>Career Objective</u>: To become an accountant for a public
accounting firm.

<u>Experience</u>:   Big Eight accounting firm.
White Dale, New York

1984-85   Completed two-semester internship by
assisting tax department and payroll
department: proved ledger column, filed
tax forms, performed basic computer
functions, added/deleted employee checks;
corrected errors; ran payroll checks.

Standard Foods/TMRS Division
White Dale, NY

1980-84   Promoted to telemarketing researcher:
performed tele-marketing product surveys
for several Standard Foods product lines,
such as Trickle Cat Food, Dormant Mouth
Wash, Heity Trash Lifters. Hired for part-
time clerical work; typed and filed
surveys, statistics, product reports for
Research Manager. Promoted after one year.
All part-time and summer help.

<u>Education</u>   Lawford University
White Dale, NY
Bachelor of Science, Accounting
Major/Computer Science Minor
Graduated: May, 1985

Job-related courses: Public Accounting,
Advanced Public Accounting, Corporate
Accounting & Finance, Financial
Accounting, Cost and Standard Accounting,
Computer Programming I & II

<u>Related</u>
<u>Interests</u>   Accounting Club (treasurer of college
acctg. club)
Math Monthly - wrote articles for school
math journal.

<u>References</u>   Will be furnished on request.

his major, the year of graduation, and highlight some courses that will show he has some knowledge of the occupation he is pursuing. As soon as some job-related experience is acquired it's advisable to let that precede education.

Experience. To an employer experience is the most important section on a résumé and one that gets better as more career-related facts are added. That is not to say you should write long prose or pad your experience with half-truths. What is most beneficial here is good, solid experience supported with details. Let's look at the sample résumé on page 146. Although Claire worked just two semesters at a Big Eight Accounting Firm, it enabled her to gain valuable on-the-job training from one of the foremost accounting establishments in the world. The fact that she put the name of the company first, rather than her position, is a way of emphasizing the employer who has trained her. When and if she becomes a higher-ranking employee, she may want to highlight the position she holds rather than the company she works for.

It is enough detail on a résumé to simply write the city and state a company is located in. If an interviewer wants to check any information with a former employer, he or she can ask for specific information during your interview. So be prepared. That includes compiling the names of employers, addresses and phone numbers.

Dates are very important on a résumé. Since being a student is a full-time occupation, you don't have to be too concerned with having dates that flow from one job to another. But once you get into the work force, it's important that dates account for all your time.

At this point in your life, potential employers aren't too concerned with your previous job titles. They understand you've been focusing on school for the past 16 years, not a career. So don't be afraid to write job titles that may seem lower level. No one expects you to be a vice president upon graduation. Explain, in brief sentences or phrases, your responsibilities, skills acquired, accomplishments, methods you initiated, promotions etc. Place the most important and appealing first; the lesser second. In the example, Claire had no title at her internship so she capsulized the tasks performed by writing the department she assisted. At her other job, Standard Foods, she not only wrote her title, but phrased it in such a way that she highlighted the fact that she had been promoted. Although her experience at Standard Foods was marketing and not accounting, she illustrates important qualities like dedication — she worked there five years; initiative — she was promoted; professionalism — she picked up a certain business sense only experience can teach.

Of course, Standard Foods is a large company to work for and will be attractive to many employers. But even if Claire had worked as a cashier at Burger King her experience would show she had motivation and trustworthiness. If she was promoted to assistant manager it would demonstrate even more skills, namely initiative, leadership abilities, etc.

Remember, it's important to look at what you've done and try to position yourself as a marketable entity.

Interests. You travel, water ski, wrestle. Do any of these apply to the job you're seeking? Are you a member of any club that is career-related? Are there any outside interests that further demonstrate how serious you are about the career you've chosen? If so, write them down. Have you any merits, accomplishments, hobbies that illustrate a skill you've acquired? Remember the gentleman who was an Eagle Scout? If you have admirable, marketable traits, don't be modest. You've got to sell yourself!

References. Although many employers do check references they usually ask for them during your interview. So you need only write this phrase or a similar one on your résumé: References will be furnished upon request. It's a good idea, however, to make a list of references now, so that you're prepared. Think of reliable people who know your aspirations and background and who will give you a recommendation that'll help you outshine the competition. Perhaps a family friend, coworker, professor will help? Be sure to have their names, addresses and phone numbers available.

Some final tips on résumés. Whether you choose to write a functional or chronological résumé, keep the following points in mind: Compose your résumé on the front side of one 8½" × 11" sheet. Arrange it neatly and make it graphically appealing, that includes proper margins. Be sure it is grammatically correct with every word spelled correctly! Write action-oriented phrases that are crisp and to the point. You may want to type your résumé and have it duplicated by a quick-print place. And for a few extra dollars you can have it typeset and printed by a professional. Typesetting will enable you to highlight important points by putting those in larger, bolder letters and printing it will make each copy clear. For the most professional look, print in black or blue ink. (A local printer will be able to help you with type-setting, since most have such equipment on premises.)

APPENDIX J
THE COVER LETTER

Timothy Andrews
9 Soundview Terrace
Cogswell, ND 58017
October 23, 1988

Mr. John Taylor, Assistant Vice President
Operations/Automation
KRANDOW CORPORATION
1010 Lanchester Drive
Cogswell, ND 58017

Dear Mr. Taylor:

Your ad in the Sunday News for a computer programmer sounds
ideal. I've recently graduated with a BS in Computer Science
from the University of North Dakota and have completed a
one-year internship where I helped design programs for a
small retail chain.

Attached is my resume. To arrange for an interview, you can
reach me during office hours at (701) 321-8183.

Cordially,

Timothy Andrews

APPENDIX K
THE INTERVIEW

Let's take it from the beginning...a potential employer has called you for an appointment or has accepted one you initiated. You confirm the date, time and if you're unsure where to go, ask directions. If you have a general idea of the location and know approximately how long it will take, then your trip should be timely. However, if you've never been to the place before, it's a good idea to make a trial run. Not only will this guarantee you won't get lost, but when the "big" day arrives, you'll know just how much time to allow yourself.

Dressing.
Coordinating an outfit a couple of days before the interview is a good safeguard. If a shirt is stained, stocking torn, a tie misplaced, you'll avoid last minute panic.

Most experts on the subject suggest that the interview outfit consist of clothing that's a step above how you'll be expected to dress each day. For men, that usually means wearing a suit, dress shirt and tie. For women, a business suit or business type dress. Even artsy kinds of jobs, that allow you to dress casually on a daily basis, should be initiated professionally. That's not to say you can't look stylish, but trendy accessories like bulky jewelry, wild ties, and exotic make-up should be worn after hours. For ideas, just pick up any popular fashion magazine. Almost every issue has an article on how to dress for work.

Once you've selected the oufit, try it on. Ask for opinions and, most importantly, pay attention to details. Do colors match? Is your shirt pressed? Are your shoes polished? I'll never forget the woman who pranced through the lobby one afternoon escorted by the personnel director. If she was hired I'd be surprised. She didn't wear a slip.

And no matter how obvious this may sound, check your personal hygiene. You'd be surprised how many people don't.

Punctuality.
Being on time the day of your interview is an indication of your punctuality in general. Allow yourself enough time to get to your destination. In fact, arriving a little early is a good way to see what the surrounding area has to offer. What restaurants are available, shops, dry cleaners, parking, etc.? Being a little early also gives you a chance to collect your thoughts and relax a bit. It's not advisable to arrive too soon and hang around the lobby. An employer may think you're overly anxious — maybe even desperate. But being punctual, even five minutes early, is a plus.

Of course, there are instances when something unexpected makes us tardy. If this happens, even if it's only a delay of five minutes, immediately call to explain your situation. Give the interviewer the option to wait for you to arrive or reschedule your appointment.

Speaking of rescheduling appointments, never commit yourself to interviews that are too close in time. Feeling pressured to rush through one, to get to another, may hinder your performance. Not only that, but you may not have enough time to prepare for both.

Additional Preparations.

How much do you know about the company you're interviewing with? If during your career search, you gathered some facts on it, review them! Find out the sales growth, product line, corporate policies, outlooks and any other tidbits available. Remember, information on specific companies can be obtained by consulting the Chamber of Commerce, the library, and by contacting the company's public relations department. The more you know about a corporation, the better equipped you'll be to impress an interviewer, as well as to determine if the company is one you'll want to work for. By the way, if a company doesn't seem like one you're interested in, go on the interview anyway. If nothing else, it will be good practice for a more important interview that'll come up.

Whether a potential employer has a copy of your résumé or not, the first thing they usually ask is that you complete an employment application form. Don't be insulted. It's a normal procedure that will seem less burdensome if you're prepared. One way to speed through a form like this is to read the section on employment application forms, appendix N. The step-by-step instructions discuss the exact information you'll need: social security number, references, former employment information, etc. And it will suggest that you make a list of these facts for handy reference. The extra time spent now will be well worth it. Not only will you feel more confident the day of your interview, but you'll be able to fill out the application clearly and succinctly. That's one more way to gain a competitive edge!

Always carry extra résumés with you. It doesn't matter how experienced an interviewer is, most ask for another copy the day you meet. But don't just tuck it under a sweaty arm — buy or borrow a professional looking folder, or if the job you're after requires a portfolio, keep a few extras in that. Graphic artists, photographers, fine artists and copywriters are job-seekers whose samples are usually the crux of an interview and usually more important than their résumé.

For details on how to set up a professional portfolio, a number of sources are available at your university library and public library.

Greeting.

The secretary or personnel clerk has just taken your employment application and she's ready to introduce you to the person who'll conduct the interview. Feeling a little tense? Sweaty? It's normal. Just keep in mind that you came without a job; leaving without one is no great loss. Maybe a brief chat with the receptionist/secretary/personnel clerk, before your interviewer arrives, will calm you? Or maybe this off-color remedy will bring relief: A friend once suggested that I picture the interviewer in his/her underwear. It sure makes a person less intimidating! If that doesn't work, remember this fact: People conducting the interview are sometimes more nervous than you. Often they are experienced in their field, but their field isn't human resources. So they're a little unsure of what to ask, what to look for. And since the person they hire is a reflection of their decision-making abilities, they tend to be uneasy.

Here comes the interviewer. Greet him/her with a smile and firm handshake. Be well-mannered, make appropriate eye contact, be friendly, yet formal. The greeting may seem fairly insignificant, considering it's a couple of minutes, compared to the average thirty you'll spend talking, but research states that a decision to hire is often made subliminally, during the first five minutes of an interview. So your greeting, dress, enthusiasm is extremely instrumental.

Questions to expect.

Too bad you can't rehearse for an interview. It might make you feel more prepared, but unless you're an actor, you'll sound pretty stale and stuffy. The best anyone can do is to have an idea of what to expect. Since no two interviews are identical, and since different methods work for different people, then having a basic understanding of what will happen can help you develop your own technique.

First point: View all questions as leads to opening conversation. Second point: relate answers to job/field/company, your background and skills. Don't rush through answers, if you need time to think, take it — within reason naturally. Here are some typical questions:

1) *Tell me about yourself.* Otherwise known as. . .What have you done lately? What are your skills? What's your background? What can you do for us?

Many people are tricked into spewing out an autobiography to an uninterested listener. When interviewers say, "Tell me about yourself," they want to know why you're suited for the job. What skills you have, what experience you've acquired and the courses you've completed that relate to the position you want. There's no room for modesty here. Be direct, specific and highlight your skills and qualities.

2) *Why would you want to work here?* or Tell me what you know about this company? Have you done research on this company?

This is a chance to show you've done your homework. Tell the interviewer what research you've done, what you like about the facts you've discovered, how your goals and abilities tie in. Be specific, confident and knowledgable. Tell the interviewer what you know! You can't expect him/her to be a mind reader, you've got to tell them facts!

3) *Why do you want to go into. . .?* What makes you think you'll like this position? What plans do you have for the future?

Remember to keep the answer job-related. No one has to know you're planning to move east, west, south of the border. Or that you want to be married, pregnant, divorced or single. The interviewer may be curious about plans like this, but it is no one's business, especially not a job interviewer's. So if you're asked this question, stick to the field and industry. Discuss your career goals, growth potential, what your plans are to get ahead.

Perhaps you're planning to take some night courses, seminars. Maybe you're about to get a special job-related certificate or license. Be honest and specific. If you've set realistic career-goals, this question won't be difficult to handle. Talk about what you'd like to be doing but show that you're open to change. If you're still unsure about the next five years, be truthful. Tell the interviewer the research you've done, the ideas you have but that you'd feel more comfortable taking your life one step at a time right now. Today you want to work at Acme company, in the Acme field as an Acme assistant. Once you accomplish this goal, then you'll look at your research from a new perspective and make more plans.

Some interviewers have a knack for asking real dillies. For instance, one of the first job interviews I had was at the headquarters of an international missionary. They were looking for a copywriter to produce articles for their monthly magazine. It featured stories on missionary work with terminally ill patients, disaster victims and with people in third-world countries. So I suppose it wasn't unusual for the two men who interviewed me to fire geographical questions. "Where's Nepal? What countries border Uganda? What are the principal cities in Brazil?" They must have doubled as game show hosts.

Don't let this frighten you. Interviewers aren't usually this tough. But be prepared to answer questions that may specifically relate to the company that's interviewing you. And be prepared for some personal, interest-related questions like the following:

5) *What have you read lately?* Any books, pamphlets, journals, tidbits on the industry is a terrific answer, and can initiate conversation you'll be well-prepared for. In fact, it's a good idea to take the time to read something relative to the career you're seeking. Then throw in any extras you've read. You may find you and the interviewer have a lot in common.

6) *What outside interests do you have?* The interviewer is getting a feel for the type of person you are. If you have any related hobbies, club memberships, activities, speak up. The fact that I studied flute for 13 years and worked at a radio station for one year certainly improved my chances for getting the job at the recording studio.

It also helps to be a little observant. In fact, if you notice something on the interviewer's desk that shows a common interest, use it to your advantage. A family ski trip photo, a tennis racket paperweight, an ash tray that has a vacation spot you visited on it, may lead to interesting conversation. On my last interview I noticed the interviewer had three hats displayed in his office, so I was ready to discuss my collection.

7) *What's your weakness?* What would you consider your biggest fault?

An answer like fat thighs or small pectoral muscles isn't what an interviewer's looking for. He or she wants to hear job related faults. To say you have none, is just as obnoxious as the first two examples. So you can handle a question like this by turning a fault into something that is really pretty positive. For instance a comment like, "My biggest fault is that I'm a perfectionist," tells the employer you may spend a little extra time on a project, but you pay attention to details and get the job done right. Or "I like people," will indicate that you get along well with others even if at times you have to be careful not to let it interfere with your work load.

Everyone has faults but revealing one or two work-related ones, in a way that sounds positive, is definitely something to prepare *before* the interview.

8) *What are your major strengths?* This is usually the follow-up question to the preceding one. What a potential employer wants to know is what are your outstanding skills and abilities that make you perfect for this position. That shouldn't be difficult to discuss. After all, you've researched the job, field and company. You've done your self-analysis. Go for it!

9) *What salary are you looking for?* Although salary is normally discussed on a second interview, it has been known to pop up on the first. So why not prepare yourself for this "tough" question?

Unless a relative owns the company, salary is never based on need. It's based on how much an employer thinks certain skills, talents, tasks are worth (and even that's questionable). So telling the interviewer you need $150,000 a year is out. To get a realistic salary range, look through the want ads to see what similar companies offer the same position, call the College Placement Council in Bethlehem, PA, call your local U.S. Employment Office, or look through library references like *The Book of Incomes* by Gerald Krefetz and Phillip Gittelman, published by Holt, Rinehart and Winston. Each and all of these sources should provide a salary range based on the marketplace.

Of course, if an interviewer talks salary on the initial meeting, you can be evasive. Why not say, "I'd like to know more about the responsibilities and skills required before we discuss salary." This is fair, since you may find that the position makes heavy demands you're not yet aware of (although it's unlikely in a first career-type position. It also is very unlikely that you will have much bargaining power, as far as salary goes, on the first-career interview.)

In any case here's a bit of good news! "The general upward trend in starting salaries of unexperienced college graduates continues, according to the annual survey recently compiled by Dr. Steven Langer of Abbott, Langer & Associates."[26]

An understanding of what questions to expect on an interview will certainly help your performance. Of course, there are other questions you may be asked: some may even be illegal. These are usually very personal and don't pertain to the job itself. The Equal Opportunity Commission has passed legislation that protects your privacy. Unless an employer can prove a personal question has relevance to the job you're seeking, it doesn't have to be answered.

What Can't Be Asked

1. Your age
2. Date of birth
3. Birth place
4. Ethnic background
5. Religious belief
6. Native language
7. Maiden name
8. Marital status
9. Date of marriage
10. Whether your spouse is employed
11. How much your spouse earns
12. Whether you are pregnant
13. Whether you have had an abortion
14. The number of dependent children living with you
15. To explain gaps in your employment record (i.e. to ascertain if you had taken time off to have children)
16. Whether you have any physical defects (But an interviewer can ask whether you have job-related defects)

Source: Equal Employment Opportunity Commission.

Some of these questions you may choose to answer in a way that sums up the matter concisely. Others you may find offensive and can certainly ask the interviewer why he or she would like to know. If you'd rather not respond you can fuss and threaten to report the interviewer. However he or she is probably unaware that the question was violating your rights. Simply state you'd prefer not to answer such an inquiry and that you feel justified since the Equal Employment Opportunity Commission has passed legislation on this issue protecting your privacy.

[26] "Starting Salaries of College Graduates Continue to Rise, Survey Reports," *Westchester Business Journal*, 4–10 Dec. 1985, p. 22.

APPENDIX L
AFTER THE INTERVIEW

Jack Fallore, of Odell & Associates an employment agency in Texas encourages job-seekers to ask "corporate questions on matters like growth potential, company philosophy and departmental structure." Ask about the day-to-day tasks and responsibilities that the position requires. And ask to see an organization chart if one is available.

Naturally, asking job-related facts is suggested on interviews, but like the interviewer, there are some questions that will be turn-offs. Inquiring about salary, vacation time, medical benefits and overtime is not advised on the first interview. Save those questions for the second and third meetings, that is, providing you're invited to meet for a second or third time.

No matter how well your interview went, an interviewer needs time to consider each candidate. So don't be disappointed if you're not asked to join the staff right away. When your meeting is over remain professional, enthusiastic and positive. Shake hands, thank the person for his/her time and if the job sounds like one for you, make some final comment that shows your interest.

Chuck Cherel, President of Professional Search Personnel in Virginia, suggests that each job-seeker "close the interview with a positive, assertive statement like: I'd really like this job. I hope to hear from you soon."

Post Interview. Always write a brief note of thanks to the person who interviewed you. It's a standard procedure that many people forget. Remembering will help you to stand out.

Then take some time to analyze the interview. Think of the good points, and the ones you should improve. Check your greeting, dress, response, the questions you asked and your rapport. Were you well-prepared? Assertive? What skills can you enhance? Reviewing these important points will help you package yourself more effectively for that great new job!

APPENDIX M
SOCIAL SECURITY CARD

Your social security number is required so that a correct record of your earnings is reported. If you should die, retire, become disabled, you or your survivors can receive benefits.

Look in the phone book under U.S. Government offices for the number and address of the Social Security Administration nearest you. Because you are over 18, you must apply for a number in person.

Bring evidence of your age, identity, and U.S. citizenship or lawful alien status when you apply. You must submit original or certified documents of one of the following in each category:

Evidence of Age & Citizenship

1) public birth certificate
2) religious record of birth or baptism
3) hospital record of birth

Evidence of Identity

1) state identity card
2) insurance policy
3) driver's license
4) school ID card
5) vaccination certificate
6) adoption record
7) school report card
8) clinic, doctor or hospital record
9) church membership or confirmation record
10) day care or nursery school record
11) court order for name change
12) labor union or fraternal organization record
13) record of membership in the Boy Scouts, Girl Scouts or other organization
14) marriage or divorce record
15) voter's registration
16) work badge or building pass
17) military or draft record
18) newspaper notice of birth
19) prior welfare ID card
20) military dependents ID
21) U.S. passport or citizen ID card
22) any other document that provides identifying data sufficient to establish proper identity. (A birth certificate is not evidence of identity.)

Your social security card will take about three weeks.

APPENDIX N
EMPLOYMENT APPLICATIONS

In the following pages we'll go through an employment application question by question. As we do, compose your own job-winning biography, one that you can carry and refer to when looking for work and one that will highlight the most attractive qualities you have for the specific job you want.

Employment application forms come in all shapes and sizes but each basically asks for the same information. So let's use the one on pages 159–162 as a guide to writing a winner!

1) Look over the form carefully and pay attention to special directions that will affect how you begin. This one says "please print." As you continue to look through, you'll also notice important areas to leave blank. These are clearly designated "For Personnel Department Use Only" or in other cases, "For Office Use Only."

2) Our example begins with a brief statement that indicates the employer will not deny you work for any unconstitutional reason. Not all forms will have an introduction like this but by law all employers are required to give everyone an equal shot at employment.

3) *Date of Application:* That's easy. Write the date you came in to fill out the form. Make sure you print it legibly in black or blue ink and continue through the entire form as neatly as possible.

4) *Position(s) applied for:* Remember my experience scrubbing the walk-in refrigerator? That's why it's important to be as specific as possible. Think over your skills and qualifications and let the employer know what you can do for the company.

5) *Referral Source:* The employer is really asking "What made you decide to come *here* to seek employment?" Check the correct box. Or if none are provided, use the choices given on this form as a guide to answering the question.

6) *Name:* The only thing tricky about filling in your name is making sure the order of your first, middle and last names correspond to the form. Most applications ask for your last name first, first name next and middle initial last.

7) *Address:* If you've just moved from school make sure you write the address where you can be reached. Your impulse may be to write your college address, so take your time. Before you write anything see how much room is provided. All too often, it's impossible to fit your entire address on one line unless you abbreviate city, state, etc. Other times you squeeze it on one line only to notice the next one is specifically provided for city, state and zip.

8) *Telephone:* Be careful to put the correct phone and area code especially if you just moved. If no one is home to cover the phone and you don't have an answering machine, give the name and number of a

Application For Employment

Applicants are considered for all positions without regard to race, color, religion, sex, national origin, age, marital or veteran status, or the presence of a non-job-related medical condition or handicap.

(PLEASE PRINT)

Date of Application _____

Position(s) Applied For _____

Referral Source: ☐ Advertisement ☐ Friend ☐ Relative ☐ Walk-In

☐ Employment Agency ☐ Other _____

Name _____
LAST   FIRST   MIDDLE

Address _____
NUMBER   STREET   CITY   STATE   ZIP CODE

Telephone ( ) _____ Social Security Number _____
Area Code

If employed and you are under 18, can you furnish a work permit? ☐ Yes ☐ No

Have you filed an application here before? ☐ Yes ☐ No   If Yes, give date _____

Have you ever been employed here before? ☐ Yes ☐ No   If Yes, give date _____

Are you employed now? ☐ Yes ☐ No   May we contact your present employer? ☐ Yes ☐ No

Are you prevented from lawfully becoming employed in this country because of Visa or Immigration Status? ☐ Yes ☐ No
(Proof of citizenship or immigration status may be required upon employment.)

On what date would you be available for work? _____

Are you available to work ☐ Full Time ☐ Part-Time ☐ Shift Work ☐ Temporary

Are you on a lay-off and subject to recall? ☐ Yes ☐ No

Can you travel if a job requires it? ☐ Yes ☐ No

Have you been convicted of a felony within the last 7 years? ☐ No ☐ Yes

If Yes, please explain _____

AN EQUAL OPPORTUNITY EMPLOYER M/F/V/H

Veteran of the U.S. military service? ☐ Yes ☐ No   If Yes, Branch _____

Do you have any physical, mental or medical impairment
or disability that would limit your job performance
for the position for which you are applying?   ☐ Yes ☐ No

If Yes, please explain _____

Are there workplace accommodations which
would assure better job placement and/or enable you to
perform your job to your maximum capability?   ☐ Yes ☐ No

If Yes, please indicate: _____

Indicate what foreign languages you speak, read, and/or write.

	FLUENTLY	GOOD	FAIR
SPEAK			
READ			
WRITE			

List professional, trade, business or civic activities and offices held.
(Exclude those which indicate race, color, religion, sex or national origin): _____

_____

Give name, address and telephone number of three references who are not related to you and are not
previous employers.

_____

_____

_____

**Special Employment Notice to Disabled Veterans, Vietnam Era Veterans, and Individuals With
Physical Or Mental Handicaps.**

Government contractors are subject to Section 402 of the Vietnam Era Veterans Readjustment Act of 1974 which
requires that they take affirmative action to employ and advance in employment qualified disabled veterans and
veterans of the Vietnam Era, and Section 503 of the Rehabilitation Act of 1973, as amended, which requires
government contractors to take affirmative action to employ and advance in employment qualified handicapped
individuals.

If you are a disabled veteran, or have a physical or mental handicap, you are invited to volunteer this information.
The purpose is to provide information regarding proper placement and appropriate accommodation to enable
you to perform the job in a proper and safe manner. This information will be treated as confidential. Failure to
provide this information will not jeopardize or adversely affect any consideration you may receive for
employment.

If you wish to be identified, please sign below.

☐ Handicapped Individual   ☐ Disabled Veteran   ☐ Vietnam Era Veteran

Signed _____

Employment Experience

Start with your present or last job. Include military service assignments and volunteer activities. Exclude organization names which indicate race, color, religion, sex or national origin.

1

Employer	Dates Employed		Work Performed
	From	To	
Address			
Job Title	Hourly Rate/Salary		
	Starting	Final	
Supervisor			
Reason for Leaving			

2

Employer	Dates Employed		Work Performed
	From	To	
Address			
Job Title	Hourly Rate/Salary		
	Starting	Final	
Supervisor			
Reason for Leaving			

3

Employer	Dates Employed		Work Performed
	From	To	
Address			
Job Title	Hourly Rate/Salary		
	Starting	Final	
Supervisor			
Reason for Leaving			

4

Employer	Dates Employed		Work Performed
	From	To	
Address			
Job Title	Hourly Rate/Salary		
	Starting	Final	
Supervisor			
Reason for Leaving			

If you need additional space, please continue on a separate sheet of paper.

Special Skills and Qualifications

Summarize special skills and qualifications
acquired from employment or other experience _____

_____

_____

_____

Education

	Elementary	High	College/University	Graduate/Professional
School Name				
Years Completed: (Circle)	4 5 6 7 8	9 10 11 12	1 2 3 4	1 2 3 4
Diploma/Degree				
Describe Course Of Study:				
Describe Specialized Training, Apprenticeship, Skills, and Extra-Curricular Activities				

Honors Received:

State any additional information you feel may be helpful to us in considering your application.

Agreement

I certify that answers given herein are true and complete to the best of my knowledge.

I authorize investigation of all statements contained in this application for employment as may be necessary in arriving at an employment decision.

In the event of employment, I understand that false or misleading information given in my application or interview(s) may result in discharge. I understand, also, that I am required to abide by all rules and regulations of the Company.

Signature of Applicant   Date

For Personnel Department Use Only

Arrange Interview   ☐ Yes   ☐ No

Remarks _____

_____
                                                    INTERVIEWER   DATE

Employed ☐ Yes ☐ No   Date of Employment _____

Job Title _____ Hourly Rate/ Salary _____ Department _____

                 By _____
                                    NAME AND TITLE   DATE

friend or relative who'll be able to give you a message. Make certain you let the person know you've used him or her as a contact. And be particularly careful to have someone who's reliable, as well as professional on the phone. I have a friend who often answers her calls, "Good Will Industries." Although she's a great person, I'd hesitate to use her as my contact person.

9) *Social Security Number:* Make sure you bring your card with you. An error in your social security number can cause problems in payroll, taxes and benefits. If you don't have one, refer to the section on prerequisites.

10) *If employed and you are under 18, can you furnish a work permit?* Unless you're a whiz kid, this question doesn't apply to anyone reading *Life After College,* so put a line through the yes / no boxes to show you have, in fact, read the question, but it doesn't apply. One line should extend through both boxes so that it's clear this question doesn't pertain to you.

11) *Have you filed an application here before?* This is self-explanatory.

12) *Have you ever been employed here before?* After question #11 this seems like a redundant inquiry but you may have filed an application before without being hired. If you answered "yes" for question #11, a "no" here would most likely prompt the interviewer to probe why you weren't hired. Answering "yes" will initiate conversation on reason for leaving, the department you worked in and the people with whom you worked.

13) *Are you employed now?* It's perfectly acceptable to look for work if you're already employed. In fact, it's how most people maintain a steady income. It's also okay to look for work if you don't have a job. But your marketability will depend on your reason for being unemployed. Employers have no trouble understanding that you haven't worked because you were in school. However, not working for the past year and one-half because you couldn't find a job, is a more suspicious circumstance.

14) *May we contact your present employer?* Potential employers who want to contact present ones, usually do so for a character and ability reference. They ask about your job performance, how you handle responsibility, if you're dependable, if you've been goofing off at your present job, etc. If you would rather not have your employer know you're looking for work, then answer "No." Let me just add, that some years back I did research for an article I wrote entitled "How To Know When It's Time For You To Look For That Great New Job." One employment consultant advised that you should never tell your supervisor you're looking for work. The employer may want to protect the company by hiring a replacement before you're ready to leave. And you know where that'll put you!

15) *Are you prevented from lawfully becoming employed in this*

country because of Visa or Immigration status? Because the majority of you will answer "no," we won't spend much time on this question. If your answer is "yes," contact the Immigration and Naturalization Department before seeking employment.

16) *On what date would you be available for work?* If you don't already know, now is the time to determine your response. Since this is one of the most important answers an employer looks for, it's obviously one you should decide before looking for work. Your starting date shouldn't be too far from the date on which you complete the application. If you say 10 months away, the employer will most likely throw the application in the "circular file" (wastebasket). If you answer one week, he/she will ask or assume you want to give your present employer notice or you need time to adjust to life away from school, starting a new job, etc.

17) *Are you available to work full-time, part-time, shift work, temporary?* This is also something you should decide before filling the form. *Full-time:* refers to a 35–40 hour work week: usually Monday through Friday from 9 A.M.to 5 P.M. or 8:30 A.M. to 4:30 P.M. *Part-time:* gives you a more flexible working schedule. Depending on the company and the nature of the job, part-time entails working more than 22½ hours and under 35 hours a week. Shift work: companies that employ people 24 hours a day, usually schedule employees into three eight-hour shifts. This, too, depends on the type of company and nature of work you're looking for. Hospitals, trucking companies, telephone answering services, etc. have shift work available. *Temporary work:* working for a company on a temporary basis means you're willing to forfeit benefits for very flexible hours. From time to time you will be asked to work on special projects that require your skills. Betty has been working for the same company in the same capacity for over four years. She's a secretary who's filling a temporary need. Although her position goes from Monday through Friday, 9 to 5, and may last forever, she's not considered a permanent employee. And she still doesn't qualify for company benefits.

18) *Are you on a lay-off and subject to recall?* Often companies need workers for a limited duration. When your project is complete and until a new one becomes available, there may be an interval where you are unemployed. Also, companies that are having financial difficulties are often forced to lay off workers. Although this may be an unpleasant situation for you it is by no means an indication of your performance. Instead it is a reflection of the company that hired you. In both cases, it's okay to tell a potential employer the circumstances of your lay-off. But if you're subject to be recalled, in either situation, your potential boss may be reluctant to hire you. (This shouldn't apply to many of you, if it does apply to any of you.)

19) *Can you travel if a job requires it?* To employers, traveling can mean going anywhere within the county to anywhere within the world.

If you're applying for a lower level position, which most of you will be, chances are this question won't affect you. But if it does, be aware that the company should cover all your living and transportation expenses while you're away.

20) *Have you been convicted of a felony within the last seven years?* This doesn't ask about traffic violations, only felonies. Hopefully everyone will answer this question with a "no!" But if you're unable to do so, leave it blank. It's better to explain the nature of your conviction in the interview. This will give you a chance to discuss the situation in a positive way. And you'll be able to clear up any misconceptions the interviewer may have.

21) *Personal Characteristics:* Although this particular application doesn't ask, many pursue personal matters such as height/weight/date of birth/marital status/dependents. Usually the employer isn't trying to pry into your private affairs, after all the Equal Employment Opportunity Commission has passed legislation protecting such private matters.

22) *Salary Desired:* This is another question omitted from the mock application on page 159. A good way to handle this issue, if it were on the questionnaire, is to leave it blank. Since many salaries are negotiable, it's better to discuss it during the interview. Of course, you can write a reasonable figure based on the marketplace but you run the risk of under- or over-pricing your skills. Since an interview is a time when you can negotiate, it's wise to wait until then.

Interviews often occur the day you fill out an application, so it's important to know what the going wage is for the position you desire. For a specific salary range read the want ads; ask people who work in the field; consult your local U.S. Department of Labor; and/or refer to such sources as the *Occupational Outlook Handbook*, a vocational guidance book published by the U.S. Department of Labor, Bureau of Labor Statistics. It should be available at the library along with many other valuable vocational sources.

23) *Do you have any physical, mental or medical impairment or disability that would limit your job performance for the position for which you are applying?* Employers are interested in your overall physical, medical and mental condition. They are not concerned with occasional headaches, nerves, infections, depressions. If you do have a serious problem, keep in mind it's a negative that may limit your chances of getting that job. Here again it's advised to leave the space blank and explain your condition, if asked, on the interview.

24) *Indicate what foreign languages you speak, read/or write.* For some jobs being fluent in a specific foreign language is imperative. For others it's a plus. And for most, it's just an additional skill that may attract an employer. When Maria applied for the receptionist job she was not only hired for her skills but for her fluency in Spanish. It seems the company who hired her was an industrial cleaning firm who employed

many Spanish porters and cleaning women. Maria is an ideal liaison.

25) *List professional, trade, business or civic activities and offices held. (Exclude those which indicate race, color, religion, sex or national origin.)* Being a member of an organization related to the job you seek, is a great way to sell yourself! It shows you're extremely interested in the field and serious about employment. However for non-career oriented jobs, or for memberships that have nothing in common with the position you're after, this question uncovers a little more about you. It reveals your sense of commitment, sociability and for those of you who have held office, it shows leadership abilities. These are all very attractive characteristics.

26) *Give name, address and telephone number of three references who are not related to you and are not previous employers.* Unless you've already done it, now is the time to round up references. Ask people who would surely give you a good character, as well as ability, recommendation. Explain the type of position you're seeking so that they can prepare an evaluation that puts you in the most favorable light. Find out the correct spelling of their names, their addresses and phone numbers. People you can ask are family, friends, professors, faculty advisors, members of an organization to which you belong, etc.

27) *Employment experience:* This is probably the most important part of an application. I'm not saying if you've never had a job you won't be able to get one. But by having the right experience you can gain an edge over other applicants.

Since you're a recent college graduate, potential employers don't expect to see any fantastic job experience. But what they can glean from your application are some very marketable skills. For instance, suppose I was a cashier at my local supermarket for three years. My experience shows I can be trusted with money. The fact that I worked there so long indicates I'm a responsible employee who is punctual, dedicated and able to learn a skill. Now if I had been promoted to a head cashier within my three year stint, it's an additional plus. This shows initiative, leadership ability, authority and trustworthiness.

Your past may reveal many of the same skills! If you've had previous jobs and volunteer activities, whether related to the job you're seeking or not, jot them down. Of course, jobs and activities relating to the position you're after are more impressive, so work on highlighting those if you have them. Write the last four positions you filled starting with the most recent first, and so on down the line. Check the dates you were employed and most importantly write the work performed. This is a great chance to emphasize your abilities. In the spaces provided, briefly state the skills you acquired and the work you accomplished. Be sure to compose it in a way that will portray a good character, as well as ability sketch. For instance, if I worked for ABC Supermarket I might write:

Handled a $5,000 till to cash customer checks. Responsible for balancing all six registers each shift, averaging $2,500 per till. Scheduled all cashiers and stock clerks.

If you can emphasize skills that will be especially important to the company you're applying to then go for it! Tailoring an application that points up your talents is a talent in itself. For instance, if I'm interested in a bartending job, it's good strategy to stress the responsibilities I've had with cash. Now if I were vying for a more career-oriented job, say accounting work, I can add the fact that I worked with figures all day. I'm certainly not lying. After all, I was responsible for balancing all registers.

By emphasizing a skill I know will be attractive to a particular employer, I will certainly make my application more impressive.

28) *The dates employed, as well as all other dates on the application.* Dates are very important to an interviewer. Elyse Bonistall, placement counselor at Office Temporaries, Inc., White Plains, NY, says "It's imperative that applicants account for all their time. One of the first things I look for on an application or résumé is that there are no time gaps in a person's profile. If you've been in school, tell us. If you took some time off to travel, let us know. Otherwise we become suspicious and think the job-seeker is trying to cover up something negative." So make sure the dates on your application flow. Then gather employment facts like correct spelling of supervisors' names, appropriate titles, addresses and phone numbers.

30) *Reason for leaving:* Although it's always better to leave a job on good terms, it doesn't always happen. If this is your case, try to write the reason in a favorable way. It's better to say your job interfered with school work than admit the boss and you argued over hours.

31) *Special skills and qualifications:* Here's an opportunity to summarize any qualifications that you weren't able to mention before. Typing, word processing, special machines or equipment you can operate are terrific extras! Especially if they relate to the job you want! So think over your past and see if you can remember some other skills you learned or hobbies that may tie in. It was easy to tell my former employer loved antiques. He decorated the lobby and many of the offices with his favorites. When he advertised for an account executive, it was a real shrewdy who got the job. Not only did she have the qualifications my boss was looking for, but she wrote on her application that she collected antiques.

Another thing you'll want to mention in this section is any special license you have. Since special certificates are necessary to obtain certain jobs, e.g., for chauffeurs, life guards, etc., detail the ones you have.

32) *Education:* Since some forms ask for graduation dates from elementary and high school, as well as college, this is an especially important answer to prepare. You'd be surprised how confused you can get while completing an application form. It's better to take the time now to tabulate your response. Our example asks for the name of each

school you attended and the number of years completed. And I've seen many others that ask for addresses, too. So why not prepare this now?

The diploma / degree column is fairly self-explanatory except for high school. Since you probably didn't specialize in any one area write "general studies" or "academic studies." For college / university and graduate school, write the degree you earned. Underneath, describe your major. Again for high school, you can print "general studies" or "academic studies." But for colleges and universities describe your concentration and any special courses that may relate to the position you're after.

Within the education category, you're also asked about any specialized training, apprenticeship, skills and extra-curricular activities. This is a chance, once again, to outshine competitors. Think over your past and put in any related job experience, as well as anything that will show you have marketable traits.

33) *Honors received:* There's no room for modesty here. If you received any outstanding merits go ahead and let them know!

34) *State any additional information you feel may be helpful to us in considering your application.* By now you should have a pretty good idea of what an employer is looking for: skills that relate to the job you're seeking; experience; strong character traits; etc. So if there's anything else, any skill, hobby, or qualities that'll increase your chances of getting the job, speak up.

Employment applications are a fact of life you'll most likely deal with over and over again. They tell an employer who you are, what you've done and where you're going. If the job market was a lot less competitive, the job application wouldn't be as vital. However, the market is flooded with people looking for work, whether they're already employed or not. That's why it's so important to package yourself properly. Review the form often and your responses too. Have you highlighted your skills? Your qualities? Have you included all job-related traits and those that will make you a step ahead of other applicants? If so, keep a handy reference sheet, perhaps 3 × 5 cards with you during the job hunt. These will be great for quick data that you can assemble for the hardest sell. Later on, if you decide to change careers or non-career related jobs, revise your reference sheets so that your employment application will market you best!

APPENDIX O
INFORMATION ON VOLUNTEERING

More information on volunteering is available by writing:

1) Voluntary Action Center
The National Center for Citizen Involvement
11 North 19th St.
Suite 500
Arlington, VA 22209
(703) 276-0542

2) General Federation
1734 N. Street, NW
Washington, D.C. 20036
(202) 347-3168

By sending a letter that briefly states what you can do, where and what interests you, they'll help place you in a position. This organization is involved in everything from NATO to Project Hope, conserving natural resources to helping control disease.

3) National Center for Voluntary Action
c/o The Clearinghouse
1313 New York Ave., NW
Washington, D.C. 20005

They'll provide information on a specific cause, direct you to a program and send a list of contacts.

4) Two national directories are published on volunteer action centers and bureaus:
  a) one is published by the United Way of America,
     Voluntarism Division
     801 North Fairfax St.
     Alexandria, VA 22314
  b) another is published by the National Center for Voluntary Action
     1625 Massachusetts Ave., NW
     Washington, D.C. 20036

5) Specific books are available on volunteering, including:

Goodworks: A Guide to Social Change
published by the Center for Study of Responsive Law in Washington, D.C.

6) Here's a pamphlet to help you assess the skills you've acquired through volunteering:

I Can: A Tool for Assessing Skills Acquired Through Volunteering
published by the Council of National Organizations
Ramco Associates
228 E. 45th St.
New York, NY 10017

7) There is even an insurance available for volunteers covering them against medical expenses, death, dismemberment and liability claims. For information write: Office of Community Development of the Governor, Olympia, WA 98504.

BIBLIOGRAPHY

Career Information

Directory of Corporate Affiliations. Skokie: National Register Publishing Co., Inc., 1980.

Encyclopedia of Associations, ed. by Margaret Fisk. Detroit: Gale Research Co., 1986.

Encyclopedia of Career And Vocational Guidance, ed., by William E. Hopke. Chicago: Ferguson Publishing, Co., 1985.

Everybody's Business An Almanac / The Irreverant Guide To Corporate America, ed. by Milton Moskowitz, Michael Katz and Robert Levering. San Francisco: Harper & Row, 1980.

Gale, Linda and Gale, Barry. The National Career Directory — An Occupational Information Handbook. New York: Arco Publishers Inc., 1979.

Levering, Robert, Moskowitz, Milton and Katz, Michael. The 100 Best Companies To Work For In America. Reading: Addison–Wesley Publishing Co., 1984.

The Macmillan Job Guide To American Corporation, ed. by Ernest A. Mackay. New York: Macmillan Co., 1967.

Standard & Poor's Register of Corporations, Directors & Executives. New York: Standard & Poor's Corp., 1983.

Thomas Register Of American Manufacturers, ed. by Ronald J. Duchaine. New York: Thomas Publishing Co., 1986.

U.S. Dept. of Labor. Occupational Outlook Handbook. Washington, D.C.: Bureau of Labor Statistics, 1984.

U.S. Employment Service. Dictionary of Occupational Titles. Washington, D.C.: U.S. Dept. of Labor, 1986.

Travel

Bowman, Dr. Thomas F., Guilani, Dr. George A. and Mingi, Dr. M. Ronald. Finding The Best Place To Live In America. New York: Warner Books, 1981.

Powell, James N. Global Employment Guide. New York: Farnsworth Publishing Co., 1979.

Pratson, Frederick. Consumer's Guide To Package Travel Around The World. Chester: Globe Pequot Press, 1984.

Remy Lois. Travel Ability. New York: Macmillan Publishing Co., 1984.

Volunteering

Goodworks: A Guide To Social Change, ed. by Kathleen Hughes. Washington, D.C.: Center For Study Of Responsive Law, 1982.

INDEX